A NEW CAPITALISM

A NEW
CAPITALISM

CREATING A JUST ECONOMY
THAT WORKS FOR ALL

FRANK ALTMAN

Forbes | Books

Published by Forbes Books, Charleston, South Carolina.
An imprint of Advantage Media Group.

Forbes Books is a registered trademark, and the Forbes Books colophon is a trademark of Forbes Media, LLC.

Printed in the United States of America.

10 9 8 7 6 5 4 3 2 1

ISBN: 978-1-95588-484-6 (Hardcover)
ISBN: 978-1-95588-485-3 (eBook)

LCCN: 2023906212

Cover design by Jivan Davé.
Layout design by Matthew Morse.

This custom publication is intended to provide accurate information and the opinions of the author in regard to the subject matter covered. It is sold with the understanding that the publisher, Forbes Books, is not engaged in rendering legal, financial, or professional services of any kind. If legal advice or other expert assistance is required, the reader is advised to seek the services of a competent professional.

Since 1917, Forbes has remained steadfast in its mission to serve as the defining voice of entrepreneurial capitalism. Forbes Books, launched in 2016 through a partnership with Advantage Media, furthers that aim by helping business and thought leaders bring their stories, passion, and knowledge to the forefront in custom books. Opinions expressed by Forbes Books authors are their own. To be considered for publication, please visit **books.Forbes.com**.

To the memory of my late wife, Leslie Miller Altman, and to my family, Miriam Altman-Reyes, Jöel Reyes, Lauren Altman, my partner, Oliver Phan, and my sister, Andrea Altman.

CONTENTS

ACKNOWLEDGMENTS

"Success has many parents, but failure is an orphan." This quote that has stayed with me throughout the years sums up the experience of Community Reinvestment Fund, USA and my journey as a social entrepreneur. In addition to the people mentioned in this book, I must credit others who helped make this book possible, including all members of the CRF Board of Trustees over the years, who saw to CRF's success even in the darkest times. Special acknowledgment goes to Warren Hanson, who was my cofounder and the first chair of the CRF Board of Trustees. My colleagues at CRF also provided inspiration and support over the years. In particular I want to acknowledge Jennifer Anderson, Eric Chapin, Katelyn Bednarski, Nick Elders, Alton Bathrick, Reza Aghamirzadeh, Chris Caines, Maggi Morse, and Keith Rachey, all of whom helped me with key elements of the book. While CRF has many charitable supporters, I want to acknowledge the early supporters who took a big chance on an idea. Thank you to Terry Saario and Karl Stauber, then at the Northwest Area Foundation, who convinced me that I should start CRF and provided the early capital to get it off the ground. Thank you also to the team at Forbes Books, especially my editor, Heath Ellison.

FOREWORD

What lies before you in this book is an insight into a man's journey and that of an organization founded with the noble intent of using capital and capitalism to create economic opportunity and agency for communities and people denied the full rewards of their labor. It is a journey of great interest to the Mastercard Center for Inclusive Growth ("the Center") where our mission is to advance equitable and sustainable economic growth and financial inclusion worldwide. We leverage Mastercard's core assets and competencies, including data insights, expertise, and technology, while administering the philanthropic Mastercard Impact Fund to produce independent research, scale global programs, and empower a community of thinkers, leaders, and doers on the front lines of inclusive growth.

When we first met Frank and the team at the Community Reinvestment Fund, USA (CRF), we knew right away that the tools and platforms they continue to build and improve upon were addressing the root issues of inequity in this country for historically underserved business owners, and we knew they had the potential to do so much more. CRF's work and mission fit with our view of what could be possible to grow an equitable, inclusive, and sustainable society because that is what they espoused in words and in action. They were focused on scale by utilizing digital tools to enable growth and build networks that facilitated the flow of capital and know-how to serve entrepreneurs better. We made several strategic grants via the Mastercard Impact Fund that resourced their efforts to build operational capacity, retool and restructure critical elements of their platforms, and build their analytics. The investments enabled their Connect2Capital and SPARK networks to bridge gaps on the ground and bring local Community Development Financial Institutions (CDFIs), government agencies, and private-sector entities closer in orbit to each other so that underserved entrepreneurs had greater ease and ability to access the necessary ingredients to stabilize and grow their businesses.

The parallels between CRF and the Center's theory of change are found in our belief that inclusive growth should bring the benefits of a growing economy to all segments of society. Unleashing people's economic potential starts with connecting them to the vital networks that power the modern economy. Infrastructure like roads, bridges, subways, the internet, financial networks, and other connected tools impact an ability to achieve well-being, prosper, and utilize one's full potential. The quality, depth, and breadth of one's connections can create significant opportunities; the more they grow, the more one is connected. The work that CRF has done under Frank's leadership and that of his team have built networks like Connect2Capital that combine the aggregate power of CDFIs via digital means to increase access to affordable capital. They have also laid the foundation for what has the potential to transform financial services in low-income areas by integrating technology and leveraging "old-fashioned" principles of customer acquisition like proximity, one-on-one relationships, cultural competency, and the local flavor that engenders and builds trust.

Equitable access to affordable working capital is a significant barrier for all small businesses, more than half of which need more funding to meet their needs. The scarcity of access to capital is even greater among entrepreneurs who are women, Black, Indigenous, and people of color (BIPOC); they receive far less financing and pay steeper interest rates than their White counterparts. CRF's success and standing in this space is significant because Frank has a proven track record of forward-thinking innovation, excellence, and unflinching resilience in a demanding industry. His ability to build a high-functioning team and organization is also a crucial part of the success of CRF. The team is always thinking about what more they can do to further their mission by creatively using and expanding their talent and capability to the next level. There is an ethos of creating value beyond what is expected of the CDFI field and building an organization that "punches far above its weight." The book you hold in your hands is testimony to those traits, and it offers important insights that will help guide all CDFIs and their partners forward to leveling the financial playing field for all.

In *A New Capitalism: Creating a Just Economy That Works for All*, Frank reflects on the hard-won lessons he has taken from a nearly forty-year dedication to improving the lives of those in financially underserved communities and anticipates the required innovations and strategies to move into the future. This book can prove inspirational and thought-provoking for all those who are working toward financial inclusion in the U.S. and globally by taking advantage of the unique position and history of CRF to discuss the history and the future of CDFIs and their role in building capacity among community lenders and maximizing the impact of philanthropy, knowledge that is indispensable in the current era of substantial disruption and transformation. Always forward-thinking trailblazers, CRF's ability to bring innovation to community finance, be resilient, and have a hustle mentality will prove instructive to others in the financial services industry. Consistently innovative, they continue to build that which will serve us now and into the future. They are successful at seeing and seizing opportunities others miss, all the while recognizing that we must be adept at developing market incentives and responding to market conditions in a manner that encourages capitalism to evolve as a system capable of accomplishing what it does best while also expanding the number of people that it reaches.

CRF has accomplished such feats by finding the means to bring the best of technology, the best of the private sector, the best talent, and the best data application to serve low- and moderate-income Americans, acting on what we at the Center herald as "bringing the best of us to serve all of us." CRF's initial approach to Mastercard paralleled its detailed attention to customers, working with our operations and technology team and inviting them to scrutinize the platform CRF was developing in detail, wanting to ensure that it met the level of quality we demand. It is rare to find organizations operating at a different scale than Mastercard that are nonetheless capable of bringing the standards of excellence we expect and similarly desirous of developing the capacity to create sustainable scale for future impact. We have enjoyed a partnership that aligns with our model of philanthropic capital, a relationship based on excellence, trust, and shared values that have enabled us to bring our best assets together.

Technological innovations like Connect2Capital and SPARK, a platform that is transforming the lending landscape for community financial institutions and banks by eliminating manual tasks, increasing automation, and simplifying the loan process from origination to repayment, reflect another aspect of Frank and CRF's wisdom that is on full display throughout *A New Capitalism*—his uncanny ability to take advantage of the moment. You will not find many better guides for meeting times of financial crisis, the very times those most vulnerable in an economy risk losing their businesses, homes, and futures, than by taking note of the ideas and experiences in this book. The ability to pivot when crisis demands is something CRF has carefully cultivated.

We hope that as readers of *A New Capitalism*, you will take action and inspiration from Frank Altman's ideas and original approaches. We hope readers across civil society, the private sector, and the government will respond and use these ideas to build partnerships that drive inclusive growth. Pursuing innovation, demanding excellence, creating collaboration, and never losing sight of the mission or the people on whom that mission is focused—these are the traits required for those who will follow in Frank Altman's footsteps and expand inclusive growth's reach to all.

—Shamina Singh

Founder and President, Mastercard Center for Inclusive Growth;
Executive Vice President Sustainability, Mastercard

—Sandy Fernandez

Vice President, North America, Mastercard Center for Inclusive Growth

*The views and opinions expressed in the foreword and in this book are those of the author and do not purport to reflect those of Mastercard or its affiliates.

CREATING CATALYSTS FOR CHANGE

In 1977, two years after I graduated from college, students around the country launched a movement against apartheid. Their campaign focused on divestment: convincing American corporations to sell shares of companies doing business with South Africa's apartheid government. The foundation of their argument was moral and straightforward, that no one should profit from a system that brutally oppresses people. Rev. Leon Sullivan, an African American member of the board of General Motors, proffered a set of principles to guide corporate responsibility in South Africa, which became the basis for a movement toward corporate social responsibility that echoes to the present day. Sullivan's principles required the following:

1. Nonsegregation of the races in all eating, comfort, and work facilities.
2. Equal and fair employment practices for all employees.
3. Equal pay for all employees doing equal or comparable work for the same period of time.

4. Initiation of and development of training programs that will prepare, in substantial numbers, blacks and other nonwhites for supervisory, administrative, clerical, and technical jobs.

5. Increasing the number of blacks and other nonwhites in management and supervisory positions.

6. Improving the quality of life for blacks and other nonwhites outside the work environment in such areas as housing, transportation, school, recreation, and health facilities.

7. Working to eliminate laws and customs that impede social, economic, and political justice. (Added in 1984.)[1]

More than 160 companies signed on to the Sullivan Principles, but by the mid-1980s the divestment campaign made pariahs of the other companies still willing to transact with the apartheid regime. Reflecting on the apartheid movement fighting for such principles, in 2010 Archbishop Desmond Tutu wrote, "We could not have achieved our freedom and just peace without the help of people around the world, who through the use of nonviolent means, such as boycotts and divestment, encouraged their governments and other corporate actors to reverse decades-long support for the Apartheid regime."[2]

The anti-apartheid movement, initially a grassroots humanitarian response, stands as a critical juncture in the successful development of what was then known as *socially responsible investing*. The movement proved that when investors' financial decisions were shaped by their morality, the impact could be sizable: changing policy, altering the

1   Boston University Board of Trustees, "The Sullivan Principles" (1977), Boston University Trustees, https://www.bu.edu/trustees/boardoftrustees/committees/acsri/principles/.

2   Desmund Tutu, "Statement by Archbishop Emeritus Desmond Tutu on U.S. Efforts to Curb Freedom of Speech," mepc.org (Middle East Policy Council, April 10, 2014), https://mepc.org/commentary/statement-archbishop-emeritus-desmond-tutu-us-efforts-curb-freedom-speech.

behavior of other investors, and creating measurable change directly in people's lives. Socially responsible investing is rooted in the recognition that money, because it holds power in people's imaginations, can be a tool for accomplishing good.

Watching the anti-apartheid divestment campaign change the world, I saw an underrealized opportunity for investors to use their money to demand change. What transpired during this period was the beginning of mainstreaming moral and ethical frameworks into investing decisions. This was a profound time in my life that helped inspire a lifelong commitment to the growing field of impact investment.

> *SOCIALLY RESPONSIBLE INVESTING IS ROOTED IN THE RECOGNITION THAT MONEY, BECAUSE IT HOLDS POWER IN PEOPLE'S IMAGINATIONS, CAN BE A TOOL FOR ACCOMPLISHING GOOD.*

Throughout my career I have sought to bridge the disconnect between money managers and the people and communities who need financing but too often are not able to access it. The organization I cofounded in 1988, Community Reinvestment Fund, USA (CRF), built on this ambition to improve lives and strengthen communities through innovative financial solutions. Over the years CRF has taken different approaches to these innovative solutions, but all of its (and my) efforts have been centered on the premise that everyone in this country deserves a shot to succeed, and impact investing is a way to help facilitate that success for many.

While I prefer the term "impact investing" to describe the work CRF does because it is more succinct and more reflective of the encompassing purpose—investments that can contribute to positive change and that are purposefully inclusive of all stakeholders—the recognized term most frequently encountered in the financial industry today for the work we do is "environmental, social, and corporate governance" (ESG). ESG is a kind of all-encompassing terminology regarding a company's collective conscientiousness for social and environmental factors. My use of the terms "impact investing" and "social enterprises" connotes an intentionality on the part of the investor to maximize social impacts while still delivering financial returns. The terms reflect recognition that capital investment can have a profound impact on people's lives and in many cases can have multiplier effects throughout communities. Impact investing is an excellent means of influencing capital markets and moving our society to an ultimate objective of a "new capitalism" incorporating principles of justice and fairness where the impediments some face in reaching financial success are removed.

In the mid-1980s, when anti-apartheid divestment had fully taken hold and before I cofounded CRF, I was the assistant commissioner for financial management at the Minnesota Department of Energy and Economic Development. I helped administer several loan programs designed to create jobs in energy-related industries, promote energy conservation in public and private buildings, and finance manufacturing facilities. This was an era when thousands of people were losing mining and timber jobs in northeastern Minnesota, and community groups were trying to do herculean work with limited resources. Federal financing had simply dried up. Without getting too technical, I had an idea for reviving these organizations by using what were then called local revolving loan funds to make loans to small-business owners, which we would bundle and then sell to investors, much the way Fannie Mae works in the residential mortgage market. The goal would be to pool enough loans to offer asset-backed securities to banks and insurance companies to buy, which would ultimately free up cash for lenders so they could then make new and larger loans to local businesses. To induce institutional investors to purchase these securities, philanthropic grants would enable us to take the first-loss position in the event of defaults.

Among the people I talked with about this idea was Warren Hanson, who at the time ran a community development corporation called the Westbank CDC. It was one of perhaps a dozen programs operating in Minnesota that had survived the demise of the Great Society agenda under President Nixon. One day in the governor's office, Warren spoke with me about the need to build a network of CDCs. Westbank CDC had run out of liquidity for projects he was trying to fund in a neighborhood that was a frequent entry point for new immigrants, and he had sold some loans to a local bank. He thought that this was an interesting idea and knew about the work I was doing at the state level. This was the era of sky-high interest rates, and Warren and I were aligned in trying to keep Main Street alive in places where people literally were unable to finance their businesses and farms were in foreclosure. Out of our conversations, we began to form investment strategies that would eventually become the norm in financial social entrepreneurship approaches. We had so much success in the pooled loan programs that emerged from our respective programs that we began to wonder why we couldn't apply this model on a much larger scale and do so across lots of diverse communities. While many thought we were crazy, working together we formed CRF.

More than thirty years later, CRF has funded more than $3.6 billion in community development loans and has served more than four thousand small businesses. We've attracted investment partners from every major money center bank, international insurance companies, mutual funds, philanthropic endowments, pension funds, and others to create new strategies and technologies that build stronger local economies, create jobs, and support economic mobility in low-income census tracts and particularly in communities of color.

MY PATH TO BECOMING A SOCIAL ENTREPRENEUR

My personal interest in social entrepreneurship was nurtured by my parents. They were Minnesota Democratic–Farmer–Labor Party members since the party's founding—middle-America, salt-of-the-earth sorts who believed in fairness and kindness. My mother grew up on a farm, and my father was an artist. They both were extremely bright individuals who, because of the Depression and my father's later service in the navy during World War II, never had the opportunity to go to college. Perhaps because of their own missed opportunities, my parents placed a high value on education. When I was in junior high and growing in awareness about the wider world, taking my parents' lead, I became engaged in Hubert Humphrey's presidential campaign. I also became keenly aware of the contentious issues the country was embroiled in, which exploded in the 1967 social unrest that burned scores of businesses in North Minneapolis. North neighborhoods were among the few in the city that did not have restrictive deed covenants forbidding sales to Black or Jewish families. Episodes of social unrest protesting the Vietnam War and promoting civil rights were omnipresent in 1967, and much of the clamor for change reached a crescendo in 1968. I was fifteen, naive, but impassioned and committed to the sorts of ideals my parents embodied.

The swirl of turmoil that engulfed the country suddenly felt at once appropriate and insignificant when, on his fifty-seventh birthday, my father suffered a massive stroke that same year. The stroke left my father disabled and unable to work. My mother struggled to make ends meet. We nearly lost our house. But my mother demonstrated the grit and tenacity necessary to guide our family through crisis, showing a strength I have tried to draw on throughout my own life. My parents wanted me to go to college, and my mother knew I shared this desire. She told me that I would have to work extra hard and earn a scholarship because my parents did not have the means to pay for a college education.

I was a good student and a diligent one, but our circumstance provided a great motivation for me. I loved learning. I liked to know how things, including systems and processes, worked. Knowing my nature, my mother allowed me to examine the contents of a special box my parents kept in our cellar. It included all the documentation for inventions my paternal grandfather had designed, including patent drawings for various agricultural machine implements. He even registered a patent on a truck that, unfortunately, never went into production due to the Great Depression. I'd never met him because he died in 1936. But to me, looking at his inventions always felt like he was speaking across a generation, and that thought stimulated my interest in invention and entrepreneurship. I was also inclined by nature to be interested in people, and the events of the times heightened my desire to learn about those with different experiences than my own.

My childhood home was in Golden Valley, a suburb west of downtown Minneapolis. At the time, Golden Valley was nearly an entirely White community. Theodore Wirth Parkway, a jewel of the Minneapolis park system, was the border between Golden Valley and the city. North Minneapolis started just across the parkway, formed of neighborhoods those of us from Golden Valley and similar suburbs seldom ventured to. This was a different time in so many ways than the country in which we now reside, a time when I wasn't allowed to wear jeans in high school. Women were not allowed to hold credit cards. The same-sex partnership I am in today would have been illegal.

Discrimination based on race, gender identification, or sexual orientation was overt and incorporated into many laws. The civil unrest that struck North Minneapolis in 1967 intensified in 1968 as a consequence of the assassination of Dr. Martin Luther King Jr. That morning as I entered my classroom at Carl Sandburg Junior High School, teachers were crying, planned curricula were abandoned, and we began to take in the impact of this cataclysmic event. I served on the student council, and together with teachers and principals we discussed how desperately we needed a means to understand our Black counterparts. Sandburg had an entirely White population and staff, while Franklin Junior High in North Minneapolis had a mostly Black population. We decided to create an exchange program where twelve students from each school took classes at the other for two weeks. I was one of the twelve selected. Those two weeks provided a transformational experience in my life. The cultures of the two schools were entirely different, and even from the relatively naive point of view of a ninth grader, I could see how governmental neglect and discrimination threw Franklin into disrepair and how scarce and dated its resources were. Like larger systemic forces, teachers at Franklin seemingly had largely given up on their students. I can't claim that I made new friendships that would last a lifetime or that I'd grown a sudden cultural competence in parts of the Black American experience, but I did leave that exchange hungry to gain an understanding of how others lived and maybe break down the people I'd been socialized to see as "other" into the "us."

Building on that experience, I helped organize one of the first fundraising walks in the country, the International Walk for Development, which was organized by students from high schools across the region. The twenty-eight-mile walk sponsored by the American Freedom from Hunger Foundation raised money for community and economic development domestically and internationally. Seeing disparate parts of the city come together for a greater good cemented a desire in me to devote my life to public service and community development. That might seem an idealistic goal for a teenager, but it is a commitment that I have tried to continually center throughout my life. At the time I didn't fully know what that inclination meant or how it might unfold, but I knew in my gut even then it was the right thing to build ways of including all people in the full workings of our society for the communities that historically did not get to participate in the upside of this country as well as the whole country. As I matured I pursued many of my natural interests and skills and realized that including all people financially was a critical means to changing lives, bettering society, and fulfilling the promise of our country's ideals.

I took my mother's advice to heart and focused on my studies. When I neared my senior year, I began to explore college curricula that could support my fledgling desire to pursue professional studies in community development, and then my lottery number came up, and I was accepted into Brown University on a full scholarship. Reflective of the social movements of the time, I entered the first coeducational class at Brown when it merged with Pembroke College, its coordinate women's school. Brown had also recently embarked on what was then known as the New Curriculum, which centered on the concept that the student was responsible for authoring his or her education rather than the institution. The curriculum encouraged students to take risks and focus on learning rather than grades. Brown provided the perfect environment for me. I learned the power of synthesis in education and of applying interdisciplinary approaches to complex subjects. I attribute my experiences at Brown with the development of the needed skill and the courage to take risks that ultimately led to founding CRF. I knew that attending Brown was a unique privilege and that I had an obligation to use this privilege for the betterment of others. I had not been born into an environment we typically associate with privilege in terms of economics, but I was provided opportunities because of my parents' values and support as well as by race and geographic location and was certainly elevated to increased privilege through the education I sought out and to which I applied myself.

While it's true that I understood that my opportunity to attend Brown granted me privilege, it is the sort of recognition that needs revisiting daily. I must remain mindful that I am in a unique minority in having this sort of educational opportunity and that I do not have firsthand experience with the inequities faced by the very people for whom I have tried diligently to advocate and for whom I have tried to be an ally—those who live below the poverty line, have a disability, are impoverished or recently immigrated, those who are too often mistreated because of their race or gender or sexuality, those who are veterans of war and those who are veterans of injustice. Darren Walker, the president of the Ford Foundation, reminds us of the very definition of privilege: "the unearned advantages or preferential treatment from which we all benefit in different ways—whether due to our place of origin, our citizenship status, our parents, our education, our ability, our gender identity, our place in a hierarchy."[3] Walker goes on to warn that "the paradox of privilege is that it shields us from fully experiencing or acknowledging inequality, even while giving us more power to do something about it."[4] What we do with our privilege is what matters. That starts by acknowledging that we have it, and it continues by scrutinizing ourselves, our businesses, and our industry

---

3   Darren Walker, "Ignorance Is the Enemy Within: On the Power of Our
     Privilege, and the Privilege of Our Power," Ford Foundation, September 12,
     2016, https://www.fordfoundation.org/just-matters/just-matters/posts/
     ignorance-is-the-enemy-within-on-the-power-of-our-privilege-and-the-privilege-of-our-power/.

4   Walker, "Ignorance Is the Enemy."

to make certain that we unearth the biases we may possess despite our best intentions not to harbor them.

THE PATH TOWARD JUST CAPITALISM

Nearly fifty years after I graduated from Brown, and more than thirty years since I founded CRF, the organization has been through every sort of economic swing imaginable. Along the way it has had to nearly reinvent itself more than once. At CRF we have developed entire new approaches to funding social enterprises, have faced down prodigious uncertainty during the Great Recession, developed new partnerships, and witnessed new trends in the social entrepreneurship space time and again. But we have never lost sight of the important work we are doing to support opportunity for those who have been cast aside by traditional capital markets and denied the chance to pursue the dreams of American capitalism. The experiences we have had with CRF parallel those of other financial organizations focused on developing social enterprises and have been shaped by continuously changing terrain in the American economy.

> TODAY WE STAND AT A UNIQUE MOMENT OF OPPORTUNITY, FOR THERE ARE TRENDS THAT POINT TO EVOLVING AMERICAN VALUES IN SUPPORT OF INCLUSION OF THOSE TOO LONG DENIED FULL PARTICIPATION IN THE MARKETPLACE AND SOCIETY ITSELF.

Today we stand at a unique moment of opportunity, for, as I will examine, there are trends that point to evolving American values in support of inclusion of those too long denied full participation in the marketplace and society itself. Stakeholders of all natures are placing new demands that markets act upon values of diversity, equity, inclusion, excellence, and sustainability. The long-held status quo belief that corporations must only focus on maximizing shareholder profits is eroding. We are living in a time when change feels possible and a new, more just form of capitalism is at hand. But nothing is decided yet. The history that has frozen many from access to capital is a long and entrenched one.

Over the course of this book, I will argue that such entrenchment has left fundamental parts of American capitalism broken. The denial of full participation in homeownership and business enterprise for many of its citizens, while generally changing, is systemic in nature and has been part of our history since our beginnings. But I will also argue that there are tools within capitalism that if used correctly can create an inclusive and just system from which all can benefit. I will examine how such tools might help us open an economy where all can share in its growth even as we emerge from multiple crises including a global pandemic, a racial reckoning, a looming environmental catas- trophe, and an expanding pluralist social justice movement. We face enormous challenges ahead, but I remain an optimist by nature. The experiences of working as a social entrepreneur over my long career continue to make me believe that, if we can find the moral fiber to do so, we can develop the tools that can create a just economy that works for all.

CHAPTER 1

AMERICAN CAPITALISM IS BROKEN

Acknowledging that American capitalism was built at a dramatic cost to many people, most specifically and persistently Black, Indigenous, and other people of color, American capitalism has built an economy of abundance unrivaled in the course of human history. By using the tools of capitalism, markets, property rights, and the system of laws and regulations within which capitalism operates, Community Reinvestment Fund, USA (CRF) has been able to fund loans to thousands of businesses, schools, and organizations across the United States. Generally speaking, CRF and organizations like it have worked to bring capitalist frameworks to undercapitalized and underinvested places. So, you might reasonably ask, why am I opening this book with a chapter on what I see as the failures of capitalism? I do so to demonstrate what capitalism can do better, not to condemn those who have profited from success in private ownership of commercial ventures or to suggest we embrace a different economic and political system. I wish instead to argue that capitalism has stumbled, that specifically the embrace by many of the belief that the only responsibility of private enterprise is to maximize profits has contributed to societal and environmental problems of crisis scale. We have too often restricted our vision of what capitalism can achieve and failed to use its strengths—particularly the role of markets—in ways that help the whole society benefit. Those who view capitalism's only pursuit as maximization of profit have shrugged off the responsibilities each of us holds as humans. A truly "free market" should believe that we all have a shared responsibility to promote freedom and opportunity for all individuals to pursue the lives, and the dreams, they desire. Capitalism has built powerful nations and potent economies, but too often it has burdened the future with unsustainable practices and used humans as the fuel that drives its engines. We all share responsibility for the problems we collectively face.

> A TRULY "FREE MARKET" SHOULD BELIEVE THAT WE ALL HAVE A SHARED RESPONSIBILITY TO PROMOTE FREEDOM AND OPPORTUNITY FOR ALL INDIVIDUALS TO PURSUE THE LIVES, AND THE DREAMS, THEY DESIRE.

MARKET FAILURES

At the root of market failures is this: in the style of capitalism we have embraced, our economic system often *privatizes benefits* and *socializes costs*. These practices generate false price signals in markets. This is true both for positive and negative externalities. In economics an externality is a side effect or consequence of an industrial or commercial activity that affects other parties without this being reflected in the cost of the goods or services involved. Let me explain what I mean.

A negative externality exists when the production or consumption of a product results in a cost to a third party independent of the transaction. Air, water, noise, and light pollution are common examples. A private corporation that generates air pollution may generate sizable profits and may provide a wanted or even a needed commodity, but the effects produced by the pollutants released may be suffered indiscriminately by people, animals, and the surrounding environment while the costs of mitigating those effects are borne by the impacted individuals themselves or by public entities such as governments.

Here is a specific contemporary example that illustrates the relevance of negative externalities to an understanding of the crossroads that exist among private markets, public regulatory entities, and ordinary citizens. In early 2022 community groups in New Jersey and California filed suit against the U.S. Environmental Protection Agency, seeking to force trash incinerators across the country—many of them in predominantly minority communities—to emit less pollution into the air. The groups asked a court to order the agency to update its standards for large incinerators, saying the EPA was supposed to do so at least ten years ago and that it has not held to revisions made to the Clean Air Act that established timelines for improvements in mechanical systems and air standards. "We've found a consistent pattern of these facilities, many of them old, being sited in environmental justice communities,"[5] said Ana Baptista, an environmental justice expert at the New School in New York; a board member of Ironbound Community Corporation in Newark, New Jersey, where one of the incinerators is located; and a native of the area. The phrase she uses, "environmental justice," refers to a movement to ensure that

---

5   Wayne Parry, "Environmental Justice Groups Sue Over Incinerator Pollution," ABC News, January 27, 2022, https://abcnews.go.com/US/wireStory/ environmental-justice-groups-sue-incinerator-pollution-82510416.

minority communities that already are disproportionately burdened with sources of pollution are not subjected to additional ones, as well as to try to lessen existing sources.[6] Underlying the arguments in these lawsuits is the recognition that not only are people who live in close proximity to such facilities harmed by the pollutants they emit, but also such facilities are often located where they are *precisely because* the adjacent and downwind communities are poor and do not have the ability to influence the decisions of corporations, lawmakers, or regulators. Lacking political capital in part because they lack actual capital, their voices are often underconsidered by power holders. Living in close proximity to something like an aging or underregulated incinerator not only exposes people to the harmful effects of airborne pollutants that can cause or exacerbate a variety of medical conditions, but it also often keeps low-income communities poor by lowering property values and not diversifying the tax base. In the terms of economics, they are subjected to negative externalities at greater levels than others.

Negative externalities often create expanding concentric ripples that continue to harm people's ability to accomplish change in their financial status. Without a strong property tax base, local schools will be underfunded. Poor educational foundations curb an ability to enter higher education and change future employment opportunities. Stagnant job growth and poor employment diversity sustain or worsen existing problems. Moreover, on balance, any positive externalities that might benefit such locales directly are minimal. For example, an industrial operation like a commercial incinerator, when in full compliance with EPA upgraded standards, is a heavily automated process, so its contribution to a job base is not sizable. Yet the presence of such a facility does not attract other nonindustrial

---

6   Parry, "Environmental Justice."

businesses, helping keep areas undesirable and the basic services required for everyday living distant.

The example found in these lawsuits filed against the EPA demonstrates something else that is important to my subject: the linkage between the environmental effects of negative externalities and social justice impacts. As is the contention of the Ironbound Community Corporation, environmental justice impacts can often be quite purposeful. That may be an uncomfortable reality, but it's not by chance that facilities like these do not operate in high-income areas where residents have better representation in political infrastructure. Social justice deficits have fewer clear causal relationships than environmental justice ones, but the impacts tend to focus on the same underrepresented populations.

Here's a common example of development that is marketed as having positive external impacts on a community. If a tribe or community opens a casino, it may benefit from the positive externalities of greater tax revenue, increased consumer spending, and a number of new jobs available to its citizens, but the community may also suffer the collective costs of more traffic congestion, greater demands on law enforcement and other public services, higher crime rates, higher alcohol consumption, and a higher number of addicted gamblers resulting in associated expenses to their families, including the costs of debt, bankruptcy, divorce, and counseling services. Markets have a hard time adjusting for such negative externalities.

What is consistently clear in both the examples is the principal investors, high-level administrators, and governing boards reap plenty of financial rewards, but because the number of individuals who benefit is small, the reach of those rewards is minimal. Meanwhile, the costs of negative externalities are spread throughout the larger society and are felt keenly among subsets of the society, most typically among those who are already economically vulnerable.

By contrast, a positive externality is one where third parties are bettered by consumption or use, and in these instances those third parties might include commercial enterprises. An example of such a positive externality is found in societies that place high value on education and create public systems to enhance educational outreach. The whole society benefits from having an educated population, which supports innovation, knowledge sharing, the production of art, and the discovery of new technologies and applied sciences. Of course, in such a society, those benefits extend to entities immersed in the market system as well; for example, employers large and small desire an educated workforce, one they either do not have to expend time and money training or one that displays self-starting ability, critical thinking, and problem solving. Education, reeducation, and training are all expensive ventures—costs that reduce profits but that enhance value and future profitability. But this is one of those externalities that private enterprise is largely willing to task others with developing. Businesses benefit from hiring employees that colleges, universities, trade schools, and publicly funded K-12 schools have educated.

Typically, neither negative nor positive externalities get priced into the goods and services that are provided by market systems. A manufacturer, for example, pays for the fossil fuels it uses to produce its product, but it pays nothing for the greenhouse gas emissions that result from its manufacturing process (its carbon footprint) and its contribution to global climate change. Nor does it pay for the impacts of other emissions on the environment, on other industries like farming and fishing, or on public health. We have not found the political will to develop ways to internalize the costs of carbon emissions or address the long history of economic inequalities that have been created by the manner in which we have developed marketplaces.

Outside of contributing to the larger tax infrastructure, as do all their workers, commercial ventures don't exclusively shoulder the price of benefits they receive from positive externalities. For example, most of public K-12 education is paid for by property taxes within school district boundaries, and public higher education is paid for through a combination of private tuition and state funding.

REGULATED MARKETS

Capitalism, even if sometimes grudgingly, does, however, adapt to regulation. In the U.S., because we have created regulated systems, the costs of goods and services do include pricing that offsets the specific costs required by regulation; so, for instance, if government regulations require systems to reduce emissions of dangerous substances in manufacturing facilities, the manufacturer passes that cost along to the consumer in the cost of the final product. Absent such regulation— and we have lots of historical examples in the U.S. among contemporary examples from other parts of the world where regulations did/do not exist—capitalism does not provide accountability for actions that cause harm. Regulations sometime provide a carrot, and sometimes they utilize a stick. For example, the Work Opportunity Tax Credit is a federal tax credit available to employers for hiring individuals from certain targeted groups who have consistently faced significant barriers to employment, while under the Affordable Care Act, businesses with fifty or more FTE employees will receive a tax penalty per employee if they do not offer health insurance. Similarly, the Community Reinvestment Act (CRA) incentivizes financial institutions by evaluating if they are making loans in low- and moderate-income neighborhoods based on examinations by their regulators. By demonstrating they are helping meet the credit needs of the communities in which they operate, financial institutions can receive higher regulatory ratings, which in turn make the institutions more attractive to regulators when applying for new charters or when attempting mergers or acquisitions. A "carrot" approach like the CRA demonstrates that despite capitalism's frequent hesitancy to self-regulate to maximize profits, it is an *adaptable* system.

Unfortunately, the U.S. has had a particularly difficult time getting legislative bodies to pass regulations that internalize negative externalities. Despite models adopted elsewhere around the world and despite decades of discussion, the U.S. has demonstrated great reluctance to institute things like a carbon tax or cap and trade regulatory programs. Despite federal inaction, slowly we are beginning to see movement on this front, and eleven Northeast states jointly cap power-sector emissions through the Regional Greenhouse Gas Initiative, joining California and, more recently, Washington, which have developed carbon pricing cap and trade programs.

> THE "FREE MARKET," AS WE HAVE ALLOWED IT TO DEVELOP, FAVORS THE MOST EXPEDIENT PATH TO HIGH PROFITABILITY.

The larger hesitancy to adopt such measures is rooted in a number of capitalist proclivities. One is that the "free market," as we have allowed it to develop, favors the most expedient path to high profitability. Competitive forces drive firms to reduce costs and increase efficiencies. I have long championed technological investment by CRF in the same spirit of developing efficient, scalable work systems, for there are tremendous benefits in doing so even in the reality that those efficiencies will reduce the numbers of workers required. But in financial markets, cost reduction and increased efficiency have histori-cally compelled banks and other lenders to focus on borrowers with good credit because they are easier and faster to underwrite than those that are perceived as having higher risk. It is "easier" to lend money to those with an established business, a favorable credit history, past profitability, and strong collateral. On the surface, this may seem simply reasonable; after all, anyone in the business of lending money wants to be repaid and wishes to make a profit. Where we run into dif-ficulty is that lenders rely on universal tools to expedite their decisions, like applying credit score thresholds. That's all well and good if your customer has access to the tools to build credit. This simply is not the typical case for low-income people, and those who have not had the financial means (due largely to systemic discrimination) to build credit scores are far less likely to possess quality collateral. The banking system also possesses an inherent bias against commercial loans to businesses in sectors that might afford someone a livelihood but that either have historically high fail rates or that are difficult to scale like restaurants, nail salons, hair salons, and niche retail businesses—the very kind of small businesses that are the likely start-ups among recent immigrants, people of color, and new entrants into commerce. They are also the kinds of businesses that can jump-start the transformation of a neighborhood and that focus on localized customer populations. Such businesses, viewed as a sector, can look risky. To instead evaluate such loan applicants as *individuals* requires a great deal more time and work, which goes against a philosophy of maximizing profits, where time equals money.

This last point suggests another default position among most lenders, that they prefer scalable businesses and large enterprises over small ones. It's true that it requires essentially the same time commitment and documentation to fund a $1 million loan as it does a $200,000 loan, but of course there is a lot more money to be made from the larger loan. Venture capitalism applies the same standards, not wanting to expend time or expertise in the support of a new venture unless it believes it will grow sizable or those behind the start-up will require capital infusion but little consultation or intervention. Viewed exclusively through a lens of profitability, such decision-making makes logical sense, but it directly contributes to further expansion of the wealth gap.

Too often investment decisions create feedback loops of the catch-22 variety, where those communities that possess the greatest need of affordable housing, new business development, or job diversity are penalized precisely because they possess need. Who buys homes in close proximity to a waste incinerator other than those who don't have a choice? Does anyone wish to live in a high-crime area? Who would not desire to send their children to the best-funded schools? Low-income and higher-income areas simply do not offer the same amenities.

SOCIAL INEQUITIES AND FAILED MARKETS

Let's look at one more example, one that is individualized rather than on the large public scale of a regional waste incinerator, but one that is influenced by similar market realities. Minnesota's Twin Cities are home to the nation's largest Somali-American population, and in one of the neighborhoods most associated with this population—Saint Paul's east side—three siblings harbored the dream of opening the community's first African market and full-service deli.

The Ali siblings—Abdiwali, Ikram, and Mohamed—had a business plan, some start-up capital, and a perfect location on a high-traffic corner in the heart of the neighborhood, but their limited credit histories made getting small-business financing a challenge, as did the fact that what they proposed was not a scalable enterprise likely to result in multiple locations. Repeatedly turned away by traditional financial institutions, the Ali family approached the African Development Center of Minnesota, a longtime advocacy resource and community development financial institution (CDFI). In turn the Center recommended CRF. Acting on a nexus of public, private, and philanthropic partners, in 2018 CRF was able to assist the African Development Center to assemble a combination of loans, forgivable loans, and grants from the city of Saint Paul and other funding sources and provide an SBA 7(a) loan, making possible the establishment of Karibu Grocery and Deli. The business immediately created eight full-time-equivalent jobs and employed six members of the Ali family, in keeping with the East African tradition of multigenerational cooperation. Karibu's success positioned it as a beacon for neighborhood pride and community development, and it has continued to grow. Karibu, which means "welcome" in Swahili, is an example of an enterprise made possible by closing the opportunity gap. The Ali family had been in Saint Paul for twenty years, but most of the people in the neighborhood surrounding Karibu are recent immigrants and rely on public transportation to reach jobs in other parts of the Twin Cities. Not only did they need local access to a grocery store near their homes, but they also desired one that carried the products and foods that are part of their traditional diet and cultural heritage. Traditional financial institutions were not able to look beyond the Ali family's limited credit history and did not come to know them or their community, and thus they could not see the important value their business could bring to East Saint Paul or the success they could realize from the devoted support of their neighborhood. Operating from an inflexible template for extending credit, traditional bankers widened the opportunity gap. However, that gap between what CRF views as the potential impact of investment and the recalcitrance of large financial institutions to take risk is fueled not only by a narrow vision of capitalism but also by entrenched inequities that are all too familiar to people like the Alis and their neighbors.

Here is how the Federal Reserve Bank of San Francisco framed this lack of equity in a 2021 publication on building an inclusive financial system:

Only recently has there been more widespread recognition that facilitating access to low-income communities and communities of color are not one and the same. Although people of color are more likely to be low income, it is not solely their income that makes accessing financial services challenging, and people of color across the income spectrum often receive inferior access to financial services relative to their White peers. These differences persist despite the existence of antidiscrimination and fair lending laws, and systemic issues continue to hamper the ability of people of color to participate fully in the economy and save for their futures.[7]

Because this inequitable access to financial services is systemic, aspects more nuanced than blatant prejudice against race come to bear. Some stem from cultural and business realities, others from bias, often unconscious bias, held within financial systems. Because the Alis formed their business in a low-income area, the investment is viewed as high risk, even though they provide an essential service and do so with little direct competition. If the Ali family instead located their business in the suburbs where there is a larger population of individuals with disposable income, they would be unlikely to attract suburban shoppers who would view their market as "ethnic," and the customers

---

7   Rocio Sanchez-Moyano and Bina Patel Shrimali, Federal Reserve Bank of San Francisco, "The Racialized Roots of Financial Exclusion," *Community Development Innovation Review: Fintech, Racial Equity, and an Inclusive Financial System* 15, no. 2 (Summer 2021), 9.

who craved their product would have to undertake the expense and difficulty of using public or alternative transportation to reach the business. Moreover, in a suburban community, the grocery would be in direct competition with large chain operations that can lower their procurement costs because of their volume, making it impossible to compete. If the family tried to locate in an urban location that had undergone gentrification, they might find a limited customer base, but the infrastructure costs would likely be unaffordable, and their core customers would still face difficulties reaching them. Neither relocation option, even if realistic, would allow them to contribute to the neighborhood and community who understood their business model, nor would it allow them to hire employees from the immediate community and expand the financial impact of the business.

Capitalism isn't effective at recognizing the investment potential of smaller enterprises and those that can actually help build community. Rather, companies like Karibu often are forced to rely on informal networks of family and friends to finance their growth. Capitalism, by and large, has failed to become the sort of system that can promote positive change for the many because only the few can meet its risk-return expectations. It also is a system that can maximize profits for a minority of individuals and corporations largely because it fails to assume responsibility for negative externalities or to accept the costs associated with achieving positive ones.

One of the things the Karibu example illustrates is something important about the nature of financial services. When making loan decisions, neither party typically has perfect information. That alone can make for suboptimal or inefficient allocation of resources. When there exists a cultural divide between the parties as well as a divide in understanding the parameters of financial decisions as they are typically made, the relationship grows more asymmetrical, which results in even more inefficient allocation of resources. When businesses do not fit narrow, largely prescribed risk patterns, the risk miscalculation may be

> **MISPRICING RISK OR MISUNDERSTANDING RISK CREATES A MARKET FAILURE.**

further fueled by racial bias, by unconscious bias, or simply by misunderstanding the business model or the consumers who would support it. Inherently, *mispricing risk or misunderstanding risk creates a market failure.*

CROSS-SECTOR SOLUTIONS

When we properly incentivize the financing of businesses like Karibu, we assist entrepreneurs who are engaged in forming social enterprises, which allows us to bring the full tools of capitalism to bear in creating solutions for the marketplace and work to reduce negative externalities. While the results of change are visible to the public through successful entities like small businesses, accomplishing such funding for enterprises that have been historically excluded from markets requires creative fundamental changes among traditional financial institutions. Change starts by acknowledging the kinds of market failures I have described and the externalities they spawn as well as by agreeing that no one is exempt from trying to mitigate them. It also requires that we see that no one entity can solve the scale of the problems we face alone. Solutions can only emerge at the nexus between private, public, and philanthropic players, what is commonly called creating a value network. At present, private enterprise is not expending sufficient capital or providing the brain trust to solve our most pressing problems, and it is seldom forced to do so as a condition of its operation. Governments are not solving these problems. And the philanthropic sector, while it has a critical role to play in social enterprises, is not large enough to meet the challenges of the problems that we must address, nor does it have sustainable funding to do so. Funding one small business like Karibu may seem relatively easy (though not as easy as you might think in the current system), but we need to fund hundreds of thousands of such businesses if we are to succeed in eliminating disparities and bring more people into the full benefits of markets. One of capitalism's aims, if it is to realize its core objective, is to "*expand* the pie" and create more markets with more participants. We need systems where partners work together and that are based not on a donor model dependent on those who feel protracted problems are important enough to combat but ones where the true cost of goods and services is internalized in their production and their regulation. Value networks recognize that all participants in them have aligned incentives, something we saw put into action with the Paycheck Protection Program, where businesses were often kept afloat by being able to protect their employees while also funding essentials like mortgage payments, rent, and utilities, which benefited not only the businesses and their employees but also the communities in which they were located.

We live in a time of clear and dire crises that ultimately impact all humans. Among them are the global climate crisis and the widening wealth gap (particularly the racial wealth gap) and corresponding erosion of the middle class. It is human nature to ignore the impacts of such crises until we know their presence in our own lives. If we have a credit history that supports our access to capital, a desire to be an entrepreneur, and an education that assists us in starting a business, we risk not seeing that many others do not share such opportunities, particularly women, people of color, and those from low-income census tracts. If we have the financial freedom to choose where we live and the schools our children attend, we are unlikely to possess the imagination to see the day-to-day realities of those for whom this is not true. Such a fundamental lack of empathy is not just common; the narrowness of our individual experience may allow us to fail to see the need to create opportunities for those whose experiences are quite different from our own.

One essential answer to such crises is to embrace empathy and act upon it through the formation of social enterprises. The need for social enterprises is by no means new. We have long needed to level financial playing fields. But we now face an uncomfortable reality. Forces larger than capitalism are producing another kind of leveling. The effects of global climate change alter everyone's lives. Extended droughts and protracted floods restrict food production, shift regional economies, and initiate large-scale human migration. Increasing intensity and frequency of damaging storms further harm already aging infrastructure, displace entire neighborhoods, and halt commerce. The smoke from larger and hotter forest fires causes and exacerbates existing human health problems and adds more greenhouse gases to the atmosphere, creating a climate feedback loop. You don't get to take a pass from hotter temperatures or water shortages or a hurricane simply because you live in a "nice neighborhood" and have secure employment. At the same time the earth has suffered climate change, it truly has become a smaller place with real-time communication, fast intercontinental transportation, and worldwide exchange of goods and services. If we doubted these realities, a global pandemic has cemented them in all of our lives. A global economy has also created global desires for products, services, and lifestyles affiliated with economic success. These forces have combined to contribute to worldwide human migrations that have made most societies far more pluralistic. In the U.S. shifting demographics mean those from different places and cultures live in closer proximity to one another with greater regularity. Our "nice neighborhood" may continue to create relative isolation or homogeneity, but even when that is the case, developments in technology and communication, participation in the workplace, or in the ordinary human transactions of daily life increase exposure to the larger multicultural reality. Even in an era where political divisions appear more extreme and more invasive, we are regularly made aware of the reactions to injustice by those who may not live in our immediate neighborhoods. We live in a moment when such increased awareness can meaningfully translate to empathy, but only if we are willing to open our hearts to the experiences of others.

Real empathy means that we also become aware of another kind of feedback loop, one where we recognize that those at the lowest end of an opportunity gap—those with the least wealth and power—suffer outsized exposure to the impacts of global climate change as well. They are more likely to live in flood-prone areas, in the heat sinks of urban centers, in neighborhoods with greater density and poorer infrastructure. And if we are capable of empathy, can we become capable of contributing to sustainable change? This "conjoining" of the social and environmental problems that prey first upon those with the least means has long been a reality. Many of those effects have been brought to light not so much through the nature of the marketplace (although supply chain disruptions and the inflation they trigger suggest there are more failures to capitalism than I've outlined here) but through social convulsions demanding change. A vocally voiced demand for change, acted upon in topsy-turvy ways at the ballot box dating back to the Great Recession of 2008, won't be swept under the rug. The pandemic, joined by long-existent social forces like the brutal murder of Black and Brown people at the hands of police, created a perfect storm for a message demanding change.

That demand now extends beyond the communities most impacted. Generations who have grown up in the post–Civil Rights Act era not only have routinely experienced greater diversity in their everyday lives, but they also are more inclined to be supportive of those seeking equity and social justice. Like the young people who were activists advocating for civil rights in the 1960s or against apartheid in the 1980s, young people today are openly expressing their support for equal treatment for all—in the streets and in social media that did not exist in earlier ages.

Is capitalism capable of assisting with making communities safer, less violent, more diverse, more stable? I believe that it absolutely could be, but all of us who drive the marketplace must insist that it does so, and then we must "vote" our conscience based on where we invest our money.

This is a time of significant societal transformation. And just as a pandemic eventually places everyone at risk, the failures of capitalism will expand in ever-widening ripples and impact all of us. Yet if we act to reverse these failures, there is also a way to improve all lives. One vital mechanism for creating such improvement is in using the tools of capitalism through social enterprise. The challenges we face are achingly real. If we choose to ignore them, we do so at our own peril.

CHAPTER 2

THE UPHEAVALS THAT HAVE SHAPED CAPITALISM

History is filled with economic and social events that shape a people and the systems they have adopted. We tend to remember such events from their flashpoints, those moments of upheaval when pressures build and build—in people, in markets, in institutions—and eruptions occur. Most students of history can identify Black Tuesday, that late-October day in 1929 when the New York Stock Exchange traded some sixteen million shares in a single day and put in motion the forces that led to the Great Depression. We may think of the Civil Rights Movement and see it through the image of Martin Luther King Jr. in the moment when he was standing on the balcony of the Lorraine Motel in Memphis just before an assassin's bullet ended his life. Such cataclysmic moments can galvanize our attention and eventually become the shorthand means for addressing huge movements that shape cultures and economies. Such moments of upheaval are frozen within us even when we were not alive to witness them.

The larger social upheavals that follow such moments are responses to exclusionary policies and practices. To assume the Wall Street crash of 1929 was only a financial disruption would be a poor reading of history and of human behavior. Without understanding the postwar atmosphere that created the Roaring Twenties decade of wealth and excess, and without acknowledging the country's prevailing historical attitudes about limiting regulation in financial markets, we risk dismissing the social forces also at work alongside the economic or technocratic ones. By 1929 the U.S. had built a culture of rapid change and massive migration by those wishing to replicate the enormous wealth accumulated by its most notable citizens. Yet, of course, the reality was that most people were restricted in their economic gains, and many others, notably recent immigrants, racial minorities, and the descendants of slaves, were systematically excluded. Just like the folly of a belief that the stock market could continue to rise forever, the exclusions of so many from the benefits of industrial expansion and personal growth in wealth created an unstable market.

Social enterprises are often useful responses to societal upheavals and can facilitate societal and market stability, even if social entrepreneurs do not view market stability as their objective. If we are to speak about cataclysmic upheavals in history that forever alter the course of a nation, an economy, or a people, we must also discuss the changes for which they become catalysts. To reveal how we might create sustainable change through investment, we need to understand both—the pressure that erupts in upheaval and the adjustments that emerge from crisis.

THE UPHEAVALS THAT HAVE SHAPED CAPITALISM

ONE MOMENT OF UPHEAVAL

As fate would have it, I've been front and center for several crisis moments. I was either in close proximity to the epicenters of defining events or they felt close to my real or ideological home. I was only a teenager during the Minneapolis riots in 1967, and my social location insulated me from many of the impacts, but my family spoke regularly about the civil disturbances that ignited in violence in our city and the forces that contributed to the unrest. I vividly recall news coverage of the assassinations of Martin Luther King Jr. and Bobby Kennedy in 1968. I was present in Los Angeles as smoke continued to rise from Koreatown in the days immediately after the 1992 riots that erupted after the officers who beat Rodney King were acquitted on excessive force charges. One of the more dramatic moments, and ultimately one that mandated readjustment of CRF in order to continue its mission, was being present in New York City on key days as the U.S. housing and financial markets imploded in 2008. The larger story of the 2008 collapse is instructive and offers additional evidence for the need of evolution in inclusive investment.

From the early days of CRF, I'd begun working with the Social Investment Forum (now called US-SIF), a national organization made up of socially minded, registered investment advisors, asset owners and managers, CDFIs, and other investment professionals with a mission of creating economic impact in communities and green corporations through socially responsible and sustainable investments. In 2008 I had been elected to the board of the organization. My

> **THE LARGER STORY OF THE 2008 COLLAPSE IS INSTRUCTIVE AND OFFERS ADDITIONAL EVIDENCE FOR THE NEED OF EVOLUTION IN INCLUSIVE INVESTMENT.**

very first board meeting was scheduled to be held at the offices of Neuberger Berman, a subsidiary affiliate of Lehman Brothers.

As I arrived in New York, CRF was in the process of closing the largest business loan securitization pool in our history, using a model that had evolved from but largely retained the principles I shared in the introduction about our approach to creating capital velocity. We had sold roughly 30 percent of the bonds in the pool. Placement of the bonds had been going well. We had placed the higher-risk bonds with socially motivated investors who were willing to take on the risk in the name of community development, yet we encountered difficulty selling the roughly 70 percent of the bonds that had been rated AAA by Standard & Poor's, the tranche we had priced to market. The AAA bonds should have been the easiest to place since they bore the highest investment grade and were priced to yield what other AAA bonds were yielding. Coming up short in closing them out and seeing that our institutional buyers were not buying, I had an inkling that the markets were in trouble.

On that Thursday in March, I prepared to leave my hotel for my first Social Investment Forum board meeting amid a week of troubling financial sector news. On Tuesday the Federal Reserve had announced a $50 billion lending facility to help struggling financial institutions. Just as I was gathering my things to depart for the meeting, my phone rang. It was Joe Stark from Bear Stearns, one of my largest investors. He said, "Frank, we've been business colleagues for years now, so I wanted to call and let you know directly from me that this platform is closing."

My blood went cold. I couldn't even say the word, so he said it for me: "File." I thought, *My God, Bear Stearns is filing for bankruptcy. The entire fund is going to collapse.* The fund, for that matter the whole of CRF, was a rounding error in the scope of Bear Stearns. We would

THE UPHEAVALS THAT HAVE SHAPED CAPITALISM

be pulled underwater in the suction of their giant, sinking ship. Was it all going to plummet? I looked out the window of this beautiful Manhattan hotel and truly understood for the first time in my life why despondent investors jumped from office towers in 1929 rather than face their financial ruin. I feared for CRF. And I feared personally, for my wife and I had recently closed on a piece of property. Would CRF survive? Would we lose the property? We had two daughters in college. Looking down the spiraling collapse of the capital markets led me to some really dark places.

There was no doubt in my mind; somehow, we had to sell out the remainder of the Series 19 CRF asset-backed securities. I arrived at the board meeting in a fog. Across the table was David Sands, whom I had known for years from the days when he had started Access Capital Strategies with one of CRF's former board members. He'd since moved on and was now the chief investment officer for Community Capital Management out of Weston, Florida.

I told David, "You know, I have ten million in senior notes to sell out of this big issue that we're trying to do. They are triple-A, if you have any interest." We weren't the only ones holding this sort of side conversation. The meeting was completely distracted by what was going on in the larger market. There were uncomfortable jokes about Lehman Brothers in the awareness that we sat in the boardroom of one of its subsidiaries. Other names of big financial institutions floated through conversations. The room, like boardrooms all around New York, was on edge. We all knew that owing to the gravity of the moment and the foundational American capitalist principle of socialism for the rich, capitalist free market for those with less, the Fed had announced the lending program for financial institutions in awareness that some heavy hitters were in serious trouble.

Once the meeting commenced, most of us at the table were on our phones texting. I was texting with David about these bonds and then texting with my CFO. We agreed that we had no choice but to reply to the market and reprice the bonds. Since CRF was at the bottom of the waterfall, repricing further reduced our position, but we needed to sell the remaining bonds immediately. David came through in a deal that was finalized in text messages with our phones literally held under the boardroom table. That night Bear Stearns had less than $3 billion on hand, insufficient capital to open its doors the next day. Three days later it was saved from bankruptcy only by a stock-for-stock buy-out by JPMorgan Chase for two dollars per share, a price no one could have ever thought imaginable.

That began a period of daily anxiety for me and for all of the CRF family. We weren't alone among CDFIs in our concern about our survival. That September JPMorgan Chase also purchased Washington Mutual, another large investor in CRF, as was JPMorgan Chase. These forced acquisitions by them left CRF severely exposed to one financial institution, a cardinal sin in investments. Chase had the ability to make or break us.

I remember walking into the office on the day in September after Lehman Brothers announced bankruptcy. I turned to Scott Young, our CFO at the time, and I asked, "Are we still in business?" He responded, "I have no idea." Scott's service was remarkable throughout this crisis, as it had always been. He saw what needed to be done to keep the CRF ship afloat, and without his leadership and experience, CRF might not have survived these tumultuous market disruptions.

Of course, our concerns for the future were echoed throughout financial institutions, large and small, all around the world. Many didn't survive. The implications for their failures and for the deep recession such failures created had only begun to hit those who were the real victims of the greed, chaos, and experimental investment tools—American families.

Ultimately, in large part thanks to Scott's relentless efforts and ingenuity, CRF survived, and while there were exceptions, most of our loans continued to perform well. Scott, the whole CRF team, and our constellation of stakeholders worked tirelessly to restructure loans when necessary to keep businesses afloat. Our model and the belief in the people and communities we invested in proved prescient, but the core of how we had done business for the first twenty years of our history necessarily changed, for similar financial tools that we had used to bring investment to the people and places where it was most needed had been applied with carelessness by far bigger financial institutions interested only in maximizing profit. They had flaunted risk in the face of return.

The 2008 financial collapse is often compared to the one that started the Great Depression in 1929, and for good reason. It represents a pattern we have lived within again, if under very different circumstances, and as part of that pattern, market regulation was the result. Part of what was different following 2008 was a publicly financed bailout largely aimed at financial institutions, insurance companies, and automobile manufacturers deemed too big to fail.

The same bailouts were not offered to those often hit hardest in the end—low-income Americans. Analysis of government response to the events of 2008 has been a critical backdrop for the dual crisis moments of the global pandemic and the civil unrest that followed a string of police shootings in the summer of 2020 that reached a crescendo with the murder of George Floyd in Minneapolis. There is no doubt that the eight minutes and fifteen seconds of video capturing George Floyd's agonizing death will remain a moment of upheaval that will be marked by future generations. Whether it will be viewed as part of a history lesson for how societies change or just another cataloged moment of continued brutality remains to be seen. But it will be a remembered moment.

THE HISTORY THAT GOT US HERE

These sharpened moments serve as entry points for discussions about the larger forces at work that have shaped our collective history and to understand the context in which impact investment approaches have arisen. In reality such moments are more like the instant of pressure release that accompanies an earthquake. The tensions that have led to those dramatic eruptions along cultural and economic fault lines were building for years, often for generations. George Floyd was far from the first Black person murdered by a White police officer. The wildfire that obliterated Paradise, California, was hardly the first evidence of shifting conditions associated with global climate change. Pressures grow over time. When the pressure builds sufficiently, the fault gives way, upheavals occur, and then, typically, when people are already feeling unsettled or vulnerable, more aftershocks arise.

From such moments of upheaval new beginnings emerge. When we heed such wake-up calls, the best among us get to work on finding innovative, scalable approaches to creating sustainable change. We say, "Never again." But it requires more than individuals. As a people we have to find the will to act on those words. As we work to rebuild our society, hopefully better than before, we start by examining the forces at work that led to the upheaval. An important caveat when we work for change is to realize that the pressure is seldom entirely relieved. If not scrutinized and systematically overhauled in full transparency, we allow the pressure to build again, opening ourselves to more upheavals and failing to create stable markets.

Impact investing is one of the means for such a systematic overhaul, and while it can utilize some of the existing financial tools available, it requires a will to say that the forces that have created imbalances for so many people can never be allowed to regather energy. Something different must rise from the debris fields that accompany upheavals.

To understand the scope of what I mean, we do have to look at a little history. Each crisis begets changes in capitalism and the rules and practices that govern capital markets. For example, it's relatively straightforward to understand that the stock market crash of 1929 literally changed the course of world history. When we look to the past, part of what we can learn is about how we arrived at certain upheavals. Equally important is to take lessons from what emerged, particularly in terms of policy changes, market responses, and cultural evolution. To understand the 1929 crash in the context of impact investing, we must recognize how we arrived there. The full story, of course, is complex, but the central theme is unfettered capitalism. After the end of World War I, the U.S. saw unprecedented growth in financial markets and corporations, and mostly it was growth absent regulation. Financial market growth was created in large part by an unprecedented explosion of technology. A good shorthand way of thinking about the scale of what I mean is to consider the "electrification of America"—the engines and electricity that transformed workplaces, labor, and the products they produced. Just as railroads had entirely altered commerce in the previous century, developments like electricity, combustion engines, radio, and antibiotics forever changed the 1920s. Having never encountered many of these technologies before and certainly never at such scale, most went largely unregulated. World history had offered lots of lessons that went ignored, for unchecked excess has a habit of creating monumental upheavals.

I wonder how many 1928 boardrooms developed growth strategies with edicts in the name of capitalism.

FREE MARKETS ARE AN ILLUSION

Whenever I introduce the principles of social impact investing to many of those who work in financial markets, the knee-jerk reaction is that it goes against the nature of capitalism. Such a viewpoint ignores something central about capitalism: in the United States we've never truly had unregulated markets, and the closest we've come to doing so has resulted in financial disaster. Historically, we've nearly always created regulated markets. Take property ownership, for example. One of the strengths of the U.S. system is that virtually every piece of property has a way of tracing ownership. From our early history, we have taken pains to create a legal framework around property rights. Of course, there also exists a tremendous irony to this history as well, for we are also a nation that enslaved people and considered

> *IN THE UNITED STATES WE'VE NEVER TRULY HAD UNREGULATED MARKETS, AND THE CLOSEST WE'VE COME TO DOING SO HAS RESULTED IN FINANCIAL DISASTER.*

them property and that, long after ending the practice of slavery, continued to restrict which people were entitled to the legal right to own property. We continue to live in an era when the descendants of slaves continue to live under its ugly shadow, continue to be denied access to property through systemically racist practices, and represent many of those who would benefit most from financial regulations that protect their rights.

We certainly have the knowledge and the capacity to use regulated markets to the benefit of all. That ability is a distinguishing factor about U.S. markets, including the real estate market. Indeed there are many places in the world where deeds are not dutifully recorded, and property disputes are common. Peruvian economist Hernando de Soto has even claimed that land title formalization was a central reason for economic growth in the United States. Titling land certainly developed a legal framework for private property rights essential to capitalism, even if it was quite imperfect capitalism that refused to acknowledge the ownership rights of Indigenous people who had inhabited the land for millennia. Today, as has been the case for most of U.S. history, when you purchase property, the deed is checked for rightful ownership, any recorded liens are exposed, and you ultimately exit the transaction confident that the property is legally registered as yours, guaranteeing you the right to sell it in the future, borrow against its equity, and enter other legal agreements regarding it. This is revealing on another front, for, overwhelmingly, who struggles the most to take actions like starting a small business?—those who do not own property and thereby demonstrate themselves as creditworthy and who have a tangible asset to secure loans against.

Property ownership is just one of many ways that commerce is regulated, whether to protect your pocketbook or your life. For example, it is notable that the first federal legislation regarding commercial airlines and pilot training came *before* any regular presence of passengers on air mail flights in 1926. Sometimes we see ahead. Sometimes we learn from others' mistakes. Imagine the chaos and corruption involved living in a country where you have no idea who legally owns any given piece of property; actually, you don't have to imagine it at all, for there are many countries around the globe where this is true, and the chaos is very real. Or imagine getting on a flight knowing that there is no centralized system of air traffic control, no regulations regarding pilot training, no requirements for aircraft maintenance, and no means for prohibiting passengers from bringing weapons or explosives on board. Absent such commonsense regulation, I suspect most of us would choose to stay on the ground. In fact, as Mehrsa Baradaran notes in her book *The Color of Money: Black Banks and the Racial Wealth Gap*, the first place where the government intervened in the economy after the Revolutionary War was in banking. Government intervention and government credit policies have shaped the economy since day one.

Every few years we do a bit of a dance regarding regulation in the financial markets. Some make arguments over whether they are too restrictive, but we have consistently heeded the lessons of past financial upheaval and created regulatory oversight with the intention of not facing the same market collapses. Individuals have many differing opinions regarding some of the particular aspects of the Dodd-Frank Act, but had many of its structures been in place prior to 2008, it's likely we could have avoided the Great Recession. Certainly, actions like the creation of the Consumer Financial Protection Bureau were long overdue and represent larger movements in financial markets that had been building over decades. Wherever an individual may stand on some particulars of financial regulation such as Dodd-Frank, the central point here is that the act was part of an ongoing history of regulated markets to bring stability to them.

In the wake of the 1929 Wall Street crash, recognizing that regulations and government deposit insurance could have prevented the rush to pull deposits out of the banking system and the inevitable collapse that accompanied it, we responded by forming the Securities and Exchange Commission, the Federal Trade Commission, the Federal Deposit Insurance Corporation, the Federal Housing Administration, new legislation for labor relations, and other measures. To ensure a competitive economy, we broke up monopolies. We regulated the stock exchange and the banking industry. While there were the expected periods of economic expansion and contraction in the decades that followed, we staved off another major economic collapse for seventy-nine years. With the recession of 2008, a financial meltdown was essentially triggered by a purposeful agenda to remove sensible regulation by those chasing maximum profits. The success of their lobbying efforts drove a willful failure to develop regulatory structures for new investment mechanisms like hedge fund trading and mortgage swaps. We had relaxed lending standards and abandoned realistic appraisals. With extremely inflated appraisals and the presence of jumbo and balloon loans, the housing market collapsed, taking insurance companies and financial institutions down with it, then starting a domino effect into other sectors of the economy. Capitalism had again failed to self-regulate. The entire economy teetered.

Who was hurt the most in the Great Recession of 2008? Unwitting homeowners who had been lured by easy access to credit for properties sold that were not sustainable, particularly those in middle- and lower-income brackets. More often still, people of color were specifically targeted. Instead of empowering them to contribute to homeownership and community progress, predatory lending practices through reverse redlining stripped the equity homeowners sought and drained the wealth out of those communities. The growth of subprime lending, higher-cost loans to borrowers with flaws on their credit records prior to the 2008 financial crisis, coupled with growing law enforcement activity in targeted neighborhoods, clearly showed a surge in manipulative practices. Not all subprime loans were predatory, but virtually all predatory loans were subprime. Predatory loans are dangerous because they charge unreasonably higher rates and fees compared to the risk, trapping homeowners in unaffordable debt, and often costing them their homes and life savings. Then, and now, the highest percentages of homeowners forced into foreclosure were people of color.[8] Some corporations collapsed—Bear Stearns, Wachovia, and Washington Mutual are prime examples—but big banks were rescued by the federal government only to grow again in the wake of the crisis. Consistent again with the idea of relief for the haves and "pull yourself up by your bootstraps" for the have-nots, that luxury was not afforded to most working-class homeowners. The pain was disproportionately imposed on homeowners of color in particular. "From 2007 to 2010, wealth for Blacks declined by an average of 31 percent, home equity by an average of 28 percent, and retirement savings by an average of 35 percent. By contrast, Whites lost 11 percent in wealth, lost 24 percent in home equity, and gained 9 percent in retirement savings."[9] Researchers at Brandeis University concluded in a 2013 report that "half the collective wealth of African-American families was stripped away during the Great Recession."[10] Clearly, this was a market failure, and a human one of epic proportions that probably would have been lessened with direct relief to borrowers. Rather than bailing out banks through cash infusions, the federal government could have stepped in to pay home mortgages, much the way they would later do with the Paycheck Protection Program.

Those at the bottoms of markets suffered the greatest. Unemployment reached 10 percent by October of 2009.[11] In the decade

---

8   Center for Responsible Lending, "Foreclosures by Race and Ethnicity: The Demographics of a Crisis," https://www.responsiblelending.org/mortgage-lending/research-analysis/foreclosures-by-race-presentation.pdf.

9   Jamell Bouie, "The Crisis in Black Homeownership: How the Recession Turned Owners into Renters and Obliterated Black American Wealth," *Slate*, July 24, 2014, https://slate.com/news-and-politics/2014/07/black-homeownership-how-the-recession-turned-owners-into-renters-and-obliterated-black-american-wealth.html, paragraph 2.

10   Bouie, "Crisis in Black Homeownership," paragraph 2.

11   U.S. Bureau of Labor Statistics, "The Recession of 2007–2009," BLS Spotlight on Statistics, February 2012, https://www.bls.gov/spotlight/2012/recession/pdf/recession_bls_spotlight.pdf.

following the market peak in 2007, there were nearly 7.8 million foreclosures.[12] The effects of the Great Recession that followed the 2008 collapse were felt most direly by Black, Hispanic, and Native American people. The vestiges of those impacts remain today, largely because disproportionate financial reality was not an anomaly but the norm. My home state of Minnesota continues to demonstrate why we need to place capital in the hands of those long denied it and why the market approaches we had developed since our founding matter so greatly. Minnesota has a high overall homeownership rate at 71.9 percent, but Black homeownership in Minnesota is among the lowest in the nation at a paltry 21 percent.[13] Nationally, the homeownership rate for Black Americans (43.4 percent) is lower than in 2010 (44.2 percent) and nearly 30 percentage points less than White Americans (72.1 percent).[14] Data gathered as part of the 2020 U.S. Census include findings from the 2019 Annual Business Survey that show only approximately 18.3 percent (1 million) of all U.S. businesses were minority owned and about 19.9 percent (1.1 million) of all businesses were owned by women.[15] Meanwhile, Black households—41 percent—are the most likely to have student loan debt and also have the largest median student loan balance of $45,000.[16]

---

12 Kari Paul and Jacob Passy, "A Decade after the Housing Crisis, Foreclosures Still Haunt Homeowners," Marketwatch, September 30, 2018, https://www.marketwatch.com/story/a-decade-after-the-housing-crisis-foreclosures-still-haunt-homeowners-2018-09-27.

13 Laurie Goodman and Jun Zhu, "Increasing Racial and Ethnic Diversity Will Drive Homeownership over the Next Two Decades: A Study of Texas, Georgia, California, and Minnesota," Urban Institute, April 19, 2021, https://www.urban.org/urban-wire/increasing-racial-and-ethnic-diversity-will-drive-homeownership-over-next-two-decades.

14 National Association of Realtors, "U.S. Homeownership Rate Experiences Largest Annual Increase on Record, though Black Homeownership Remains Lower Than a Decade Ago, NAR Analysis Finds," February 22, 2022, https://www.nar.realtor/newsroom/u-s-homeownership-rate-experiences-largest-annual-increase-on-record-though-black-homeownership-remains-lower-than-decade-ago.

15 United States Census Bureau, "Annual Business Survey Release Provides Data on Minority-Owned, Veteran-Owned and Women-Owned Businesses," January 28, 2021, https://www.census.gov/newsroom/press-releases/2021/annual-business-survey.html.

16 National Association of Realtors, "U.S. Homeownership Rate."

While the Great Recession impacted Black people and other minorities disproportionately, this market upheaval represented a frequent pattern where racial bias is systemic in the very methodologies and rules within financial markets, particularly in banking. It also demonstrates a pattern whereby the industries being regulated by federal and state agencies gain control of the regulators, ensuring the means to continue imbalanced opportunities for wealth creation.

There is a long history to these patterns. The accountability developed in regulatory responses to the lessons of 1929 gradually gave way to the power of political currency. We've seen the pattern repeat itself in terms of environmental policy as well. The first federal environmental law, the National Environmental Policy Act, signed into law in 1970, mandated that federal agencies consider environmental impact as one factor when making decisions and included the formation of the Environmental Protection Agency, an agency that President Trump vowed to abolish. The responses of the 1970s to a series of environmental crises that had been building for decades established the Clean Air Act and the Clean Water Act, yet the regulations that emerged from those laws continue to be watered down as industries lobby politicians and gain representation within the regulatory bodies themselves. Legislators created subsidies for the oil and gas industries. The tax code has been modified repeatedly. With the Trump presidency, we witnessed a wholesale attempt to gut the agencies that regulate industries that are central contributors to environmental degradation. This has been part of a steady drumbeat, typically sung to the tune of "free markets." We witness the result when too much regulation is pulled back in catastrophes like the Flint water crisis, which is an important example of a tragedy that can and will be repeated in communities across the country if we concede only to the narrow interests of free-market enthusiasts. It has an equivalent to the kinds of structural inequities that allow homeowners associations to create discriminatory policies and by zoning decisions that create quilt-like patterns of unequal wealth. Moreover, there is a direct correlation to the kinds of negligence and overt denial of responsibility present in the environmental and public health emergency present in Flint and the disproportionate impacts on minority communities; it should be of little surprise that Flint is overwhelmingly a Black community.

"FREE MARKET" FAILURES AND IMPERFECT REGULATION

I have devoted my career to supporting investment in communities that often look a lot like Flint, Michigan. In order to fully explicate the impact inclusive capitalism can have in transforming such places, it's helpful to turn to a little broader history about the rise of social justice movements in response to more than two centuries of inequity.

Both sides of the equation I introduced with regard to environmental concerns—manipulations of tax code, agency oversight, etc. and the presence of regulation to look out for the common good—suggest the reality that we've not had unfettered markets in regard to environmental impact for more than fifty years. And, as the formation of key policies and federal agencies after the Great Depression attests, we have not had unfettered financial markets for nearly one hundred years. Yet we have still managed to experience unprecedented growth throughout financial markets, witnessed new industries emerge, benefited as new jobs have been created, and marveled as new technologies arose, all to fuel what is now a truly global marketplace with the United States leading the way. Capitalism has done just fine. The real problem with regulation is that it has now created a framework of rules that favor some and disadvantage others. What we need is not unfettered capitalism but fair markets that are inclusive.

But, of course, capitalism has always been imperfect. Each generation is forced to confront the shortcomings of capitalism in its own way, identifying inequity and crisis that the majority in past generations of capitalists dismissed as the cost of doing business. I hope that my legacy will be helping to build some of the climate within finance that has incubated the generation that has entered the workforce over the past ten to twenty years where more and more individuals are focused on fixing the shortcomings of capitalism through social enterprise.

> THE REAL PROBLEM WITH REGULATION IS THAT IT HAS NOW CREATED A FRAMEWORK OF RULES THAT FAVOR SOME AND DISADVANTAGE OTHERS. WHAT WE NEED IS NOT UNFETTERED CAPITALISM BUT FAIR MARKETS THAT ARE INCLUSIVE.

There is a lot to fix. The inequities that created the catastrophic collapse of Black wealth we saw with the Great Recession have been in place since before the founding of the nation and have been deeply and systematically entrenched in financial systems throughout our country's history. Yet, and the irony is not lost, one could argue that it was "America's original sin," as James Madison put it—slavery—that created the foundations of modern American capitalism. Mehrsa Baradaran, a professor of banking law and the author of *The Color of Money*, reminds us that "the effects of the institution of slavery on American commerce were monumental—3.2 million slaves were worth $1.3 billion in market value, almost equal to the entire gross national product."[17] She goes on to remind us that slaves "were liquid assets that could be exchanged on markets more easily than other forms of property."[18] For most, the end of slavery was a formality and not a reality, and this was certainly reflected in restrictions for Black financial opportunity. In the Reconstruction era, most freed slaves were left landless and voteless, and many states passed laws forbidding people of color to take up trades or occupations, and they blocked access to higher education, leaving most with no choice but to grow cotton. Locked out of the Homestead Act and excluded from private property ownership in many Southern states, most served as indentured servants or sharecropped, working for a landlord rather than an owner but to the same effect. As Baradaran writes, "The myth that free-market principles were guiding political choices was further exposed as hypocrisy because blacks could not even pay 'market prices' for land. White southerners simply refused to sell land to blacks."[19] Many Southern states formalized such refusal and passed laws that made it illegal for White sellers to sell land to Blacks. Even in devising the legislation passed as part of the New Deal, the Southern bloc excluded farmers and domestic workers—the primary occupations for most Southern Blacks at the time—from regulated work hours, union representation, minimum wage requirements, and Social Security benefits.

Indeed, it was racial discrimination in mortgage lending as practiced in the 1930s that still shapes the demographic and wealth patterns of American communities today, with three out of four of the neighborhoods "redlined" on government maps eighty years ago con-

---

17   Mehrsa Baradaran, *The Color of Money: Black Banks and the Racial Wealth Gap* (Cambridge, MA: Belknap Press, 2019).

18   Baradaran, *Color of Money.*

19   Baradaran, *Color of Money.*

tinuing to struggle economically.[20] In the 1930s government surveyors graded neighborhoods in 239 cities, color-coding them green for "best," blue for "still desirable," yellow for "definitely declining," and red for "hazardous." Local lenders discounted "redlined" areas as credit risks, in large part because of the residents' racial and ethnic demographics. Neighborhoods that were predominantly made up of Black people, as well as religious minorities like Catholics, Jews, and immigrants from Asia and southern Europe, were deemed undesirable. Loans in redlined neighborhoods were often entirely unavailable and when available were more expensive. The Federal Housing Administration institutionalized the system of discriminatory lending by developing government-backed mortgages, reflecting local race-based criteria in their underwriting practices and reinforcing residential segregation in American cities. Those who possessed wealth used the materials available—commerce, credit, money, and segregation—to regenerate inequality. Redlining practices were not made illegal until 1968 with the passage of the Fair Housing Act. Yet de facto redlining still exists, with mortgage providers blaming loan nonapproval on poor FICO scores (which, it's worth noting, did not exist before 1989). A 2018 report by the Center for Investigative Reporting showed that "redlining persists in sixty-one metro areas—from Detroit and Philadelphia to Little Rock and Tacoma—even when controlling for applicants' income, loan amount and neighborhood, according to its analysis of Home Mortgage Disclosure Act records."[21] Redlining in 1930 and redlining today are just another mechanism of exclusionary laws and lending practices that starve homeowners and entrepreneurs of color from access to credit.

---

20   Tracy Jan, "Redlining Was Banned 50 Years Ago. It's Still Hurting Minorities Today," *Washington Post*, March 28, 2018, https://www.washingtonpost.com/news/wonk/wp/2018/03/28/redlining-was-banned-50-years-ago-its-still-hurting-minorities-today/.

21   Jan, "Redlining Was Banned."

Part of the logic of capitalism is that it wants to build as many profitable business lines as possible, and that potentially leaves more and more people out of the system, perhaps not intentionally, but as a result of only valuing high profits and ones that are easily achieved. Discriminatory practices may or may not be purposeful and they may be unconscious, yet they always reveal the prevailing values of the times. Capitalism's shortcomings are exposed in different ways in different times. But a consistent area where capitalism fails us, in general, has been its propensity to view people as commodities and tools. Our nation's history reminds us that at its worst capitalism has treated people as property. Slavery's presence was justified by a capitalistic economic argument that in an agrarian economy, the market required a tool to minimize labor costs. The human costs of slavery remain something that our country has never truly reckoned with or fully acknowledged.

The dependency in agriculture to utilize the cheapest labor force possible remains with us today as in seen in the dependency on the use of migrant laborers. We are still willing to pay wages far lower than market norms to drive profits whether that labor is performed by migrants in the U.S. or by moving manufacturing abroad. Even at the most forgiving end of the spectrum of a market vision toward people, we may want to please our "customers," but in the big data of a large enterprise, customers are a data set, not individuals. We may see it as important to retain our "workforce," but ultimately labor is a critical item on a profit and loss statement, one of the most expensive cost categories of all.

Consider a historical example from my hometown, one that was repeated throughout the U.S. In the 1950s, as suburbs became more popular and commerce grew into new expanded markets at greater distances, we developed the interstate highway system and other transportation infrastructure. In the Twin Cities, this included the development of Interstate 94. The path for I-94 is a classic example of not-in-my-backyard applications of capitalism. Whose shouts of NIMBY have the least amplification? The neighborhoods north and south of Rondo Avenue, extending south into today's Summit-University neighborhood and north to University Avenue, were always diverse. By the 1950s about 85 percent of Saint Paul's Black population lived in these neighborhoods, often collectively referred to as "Rondo." The freeway location chosen in 1956 along Saint Anthony Avenue took out most of Rondo and divided what was left. More than six hundred Black families, alongside numerous businesses and institutions, lost their homes. Today there is a movement forming that wishes to build a billion-dollar bridge across the interstate to reconnect those fractured neighborhoods. What started as a grassroots movement has gained traction because moral values have shifted, and the project has the support of diverse people far beyond the neighborhoods immediately affected.

The movement to rebuild or reconnect communities we are seeing in the Twin Cities is being repeated around the country, perhaps most visibly in Los Angeles. There, like in Minneapolis and elsewhere, these attempts to rebuild communities are quite distinct from other powerful economic movements that result in gentrification. In instances of gentrification, those who are displaced, which is nearly always low-income residents, must go somewhere. Their pain is real, as is the fracture that happens in what were once their communities. When we invest in those who are members of neighborhood communities rather than displacing them in pursuit of the new vogue arts community or hipster nightlife, we strengthen the fabric of those communities and provide jobs to those who might turn to black-market activities to generate income.

A great model is found in Homeboy Industries in East Los Angeles. Homeboy was started in 1988 by Father Gregory Boyle after he became the pastor of Delores Mission Church in what was then the poorest parish in Los Angeles and home to two of the largest public housing projects west of the Mississippi. What began as a way of improving the lives of people formerly affiliated with gangs has evolved into the largest gang intervention, rehabilitation, and reentry program in the world. By investing in Homeboy, those who were often left behind without hope have had their lives transformed, impacting the lives of their families and community and creating a ripple effect all around Los Angeles and beyond. Father Greg popularized the radical notion that even the most demonized individuals can thrive when given a second (or in some cases a first) chance. From the outset he partnered with local Los Angeles businesses in the Boyle Heights neighborhood, encouraging them to hire participants in the program. Eventually, Homeboy was established as a nonprofit and began creating and operating its own job training businesses. Now, Homeboy has grown from a single bakery to almost a dozen social enterprises that provide both a vital training ground for clients as well as revenue streams to support the mission. Homeboy and numerous other grassroots programs offer ready testimony that people can transcend their pasts and become valuable, empowered community members, employees, and business leaders.

Organizations like Homeboy had developed the community ties, financial expertise, and social entrepreneurship skills to help create a path toward reconstruction and reconnection in 1992 in the wake of the civil disturbances following the acquittal of four Los Angeles police officers on charges of beating Rodney King. Like similar more recent incidents, the Rodney King beating was videotaped, galvanizing people's attention worldwide. While having a video record of such an incident was highly unusual in 1992, it was a harbinger of our current environment where with the omnipresence of cell phones and video-sharing applications, more police actions are widely and immediately distributed for viewing by anyone who is interested. The kinds of actions that culminated in the 1955 lynching of Emmett Till or the 1963 murder of Medgar Evers and speculated about in the press or hinted at in court documents are now often documented with visual proof and broadcast, often in real time. While one direction of flow has been to bring such incidents into open public discourse, the counterflow, one brought on by gains in inclusion among our culture generally, has been to move such incidents more often from actions of *clearly* racist intent to subtler but no less deadly extensions of systemic racism that reflect complex and frequently unacknowledged vestiges of exclusionary belief systems.

I was present in Los Angeles days after the riots ended. The trip to California represented a big moment for CRF because I was scouting California for expansion of our loan programs outside of our home area. I was touring California and introducing myself to those in the civic, community development, and philanthropic spaces and talking about what CRF was doing. Smoke was still literally rising from many of the thousands of businesses that were lost or ruined in the uprising. I was able to get a meeting with city officials, which was held in the Koreatown section of South Central Los Angeles, and the building where we met had all of its main floor windows boarded up where the glass had been broken. Among the people I met at the meeting was Michael Banner, who later became a long-serving board member at CRF and at the time was a consultant for the city. Michael was a banking executive specializing in commercial loans and had developed an extensive background utilizing public funds to stimulate revitalization in what were then called "distressed neighborhoods." Meeting

Michael and seeing firsthand the devastation to the community that arose from the disenfranchisement of its citizens that the Rodney King case had made so visually clear saddened me greatly but also motivated me to redouble our efforts to use capital to create real change. Out of conversations that started at that meeting, I learned about Michael's efforts to ramp up the activities of the Los Angeles Local Development Corporation and his work creating ways to finance small businesses and nonprofits primarily in Black neighborhoods of LA. CRF became the source of their liquidity. One of the early loans that we purchased from Los Angeles LDC was a loan to Homeboy Industries. Thirty years after the upheavals that had destroyed so much of the Koreatown neighborhood, it is now a largely gentrified section of the city and one of the most diverse neighborhoods in Los Angeles, home to a vibrant nightlife and a growing tech hub.

The visions of Koreatown as I saw it in 1992 stay with me. Those visions were reignited in 2020 when violence and destruction erupted in places that I know intimately at home in Minneapolis in the aftermath of George Floyd's murder. His murder felt very personal to me, for not only was he a member of the community where I live, but the scene of his murder, less than two miles from our offices, is also in the heart of neighborhoods where CRF and other CDFIs have made hundreds of loans following the kind of model we had used in LA. As I watched the Black Lives Matter protests spark similar outrage all across the globe, I knew the stakes had been raised again and that CRF needed to do its part in rebuilding the community. But his murder had shaken me, my staff, and my board, and we needed ways to deal with the emotions we were feeling. Many members of our team felt a need for a safe place to grieve and share their experiences. Within hours the CRF staff organized a call that we all joined. We cried together, and we learned from each other. That call has been institutionalized at CRF in recurring diversity, equity, and inclusion (DEI) calls, which sometimes include guests, to build understanding and to explore the range of issues and opportunities in DEI. Among the first people I turned to for advice was Michael Banner. He immediately responded and said that he'd be happy to join our DEI call. Specifically, he would speak to his own experience of having his brother killed by police. His was a personalization of the injustice I could not imagine. Michael was not only uniquely qualified to address the emotions released by seminal moments like George Floyd's murder, but he had also spent most of his professional life helping rebuild communities in the aftermath of such tragedy.

I have no doubt that the collision of disparate events will mark 2020 as a period of upheaval that will forever reshape the economic, cultural, and political landscape of the U.S. What new contours might look like, as well as a closer examination of the forces that created such upheaval, will be the focus of important later sections of this book. But first, to understand the solutions that emerge out of economic and social upheavals, we need to recognize forces at work that are creating trends in support of social entrepreneurs spearheading such solutions. Then I need to share more on how the CDFI industry works, define what social enterprises are and show you them in action, and address how they manage risk to benefit people on all sides of a transaction.

When we face upheavals, both those of the market and those that arise from social issues, the message is the same: we shouldn't go back to the way we were doing it before. As we move forward, we not only need to understand the implications of what went wrong; we need to make sure that new approaches to innovation don't block out the very people most adversely affected. That which is at stake if we maintain "same as we've always done" practices goes far beyond bad implications for people and communities with fewer resources.

Unless we address the fault lines present in global climate change and in the inequitable dispersal of opportunity within our financial systems, we cannot ensure protection of the unalienable rights of life, liberty, and the pursuit of happiness as promised by our democracy. Investments in social enterprises contain a vital means for addressing these fault lines, but they cannot work on their own. Just as we have to understand the larger context of history to understand the pivotal, flashpoint moments that enter collective memory, to make social investment enterprises promote lasting progress requires a fundamental will to change at foundational levels of institutional practices and necessitates a cohesion of social, political, and economic forces.

CHAPTER 3

EMERGING TRENDS SHAPING CAPITALISM

Investing in social enterprises is not new. In colonial times, settlers of Jamestown were employees of the Virginia Company, and investors in that company controlled all the English land claims for the colony. All the colonies expanded from land grants, often received directly from the Crown. Such arrangements were public/private engagements that looked to governments, companies, and individuals alike as effective ways to expand economic opportunity and create wealth. It should be noted that these arrangements were exceptionally problematic and entirely disregarded the rights of Indigenous peoples—a recurring theme present in many later public/private engagements. The patterns of such expansion (at the expense of people already living in places marked for colonial development) were largely replicated through nearly all land acquisition for railroads and canals and in the Homestead Act. Even the latter massive economic experiment may seem far flung from the formation of agricultural co-ops, fraternal common bond institutions, mutual life insurance companies, or the organization of labor unions to purchase affordable housing or finance healthcare facilities, just some of the practices that certainly were early actions of social enterprise.

These public/private partnerships have, of course, evolved in complex ways and have undergone numerous experiments. Today, at the center point of public/private/philanthropic collaboration, there is growing discussion about the need to address the kinds of inequities that spark societal upheavals I discussed in the previous chapter. Simultaneously, there is greater demand from a wider range of the world's citizenry for governments and corporations alike to address global climate change. Contemporary upheavals have fueled those discussions and made the need for change appear more pressing. A growing number of laypeople throughout society are taking greater and greater interest in what once were considered the problems faced by a minority of the population. More people have begun to recognize the fragility present in capitalism through the hard economic lessons of the COVID-19 pandemic, the sustainability problems brought on by dependence on fossil fuels and the imbalances they create in living ecosystems, and the legacy of inequitable economic realities for people of color. The topic of a wealth gap between the very richest individuals and the remainder of the population, both in the hard facts of a shrinking middle class and a growing impoverished class, has moved from a fringe topic to a central platform item in political races. The growth of the social justice movement increasingly is no longer seen as a problem impacting specific segments of society but something everyone should be concerned about. At the same time leaders of social justice movements have found far more allies, they have grown in their organizational abilities and political power, and they are now seizing a moment when the public is better prepared to understand the systemic nature of inequitable treatment for those who have long been marginalized. Simultaneously, just as a more enlightened public awakens to the demands by those heralding social justice reform, dramatic and frequent natural disasters command attention to a changing climate. Increasingly, those advocating for social justice and those advocating for change to combat the climate crisis are beginning to recognize the crossover effects of their movements and understand that those throughout the world suffering the greatest consequences of climate change are lower-income communities and those who are most vulnerable to political and economic instability.

An additional result of growing public consciousness and call for action on these issues is an interest in the ways that social enterprise can be used to address needed transformation. Considering environmental impact in investment decisions is well underway. The social aspects of ESG are more nascent in their development, but one trend that is taking hold is the creation of social enterprise aimed at creating greater access to capital. The potential embrace of this trend is best epitomized in the action taken by Business Roundtable in August of 2019, when it issued a document that redefined the purpose of a corporation as one that promotes "an economy that serves all Americans,"[22] a clear movement away from shareholder primacy. The statement was signed by 181 CEOs who committed to lead their companies for "the benefit of all stakeholders—customers, employees, suppliers, communities and shareholders."[23] The Business Roundtable statement has brought more mainstream corporations to recognize the value of and the public interest in developing intentionality in

---

22   Business Roundtable, "Business Roundtable Redefines the Purpose of a Corporation to Promote 'An Economy That Serves All Americans,'" August 19, 2019, https://www.businessroundtable.org/business-roundtable-redefines-the-purpose-of-a-corporation-to-promote-an-economy-that-serves-all-americans.

23   Business Roundtable, "Business Roundtable Redefines."

corporate ESG commitments. It has, providing little surprise in an age of bifurcated politics, drawn ridicule from others.

While I am an optimist by nature, if you allow me a moment of pessimism, the increasing regularity with which those in some quarters pen troubled editorials about the presence of ESG within financial institutions processes or push for legislative action to punish such institutions for applying ESG data suggests growing awareness of ESG as a factor in investment decisions. An extreme example of such concern is demonstrated by a 2022 decision by West Virginia to bar five major financial institutions from entering into banking contracts with the state treasurer's office or any state agency on claims that they were using ESG standards to push anti–fossil fuel policies.[24]

As a nation we may be split on matters like ESG reporting or policy application; however, I would argue that like so many social issues, polling among the populace suggests a far more public embrace of environmental and social justice principles than might be visible from a narrow political lens or from mass media coverage on such issues. The very fact that, from opposing perspectives, such topics are at the center of public, political, and boardroom discourse suggests that ESG concerns have passed the "trend" threshold.

Indeed, I would argue that the COVID-19 global pandemic and turmoil accompanying protests in the wake of George Floyd's murder on May 25, 2020, demonstrate that we have reached a seminal moment for those demanding change (and perhaps those most resistant to it as well). As I will chronicle in greater detail in the following chapter, George Floyd's murder took place in a neighborhood of Minneapolis where a good deal of private, public, and

---

24   Thomas Catenacci, "Republican States Are Planning an All-Out Assault on Woke Banks: 'We Won't Do Business with You,'" *Fox Business*, August 4, 2022, https://www.foxbusiness.com/politics/republican-states-planning-assault-woke-banks-wont-do-business.

philanthropic partnership collaborations had invested. When peaceful protests decrying his murder eventually spilled over into anger and frustration, many of the entrepreneurs incubated by these cross-sector collaborations suffered damage and financial hardship. This came in a historic moment of unprecedented economic upheaval when they, like businesses across the globe, were already feeling the difficulties brought on by COVID-19 closures and staffing issues.

Two years later numerous questions still emerge from these events. Will investors wishing to help promote social ventures reinvest once more? Can business owners find the resiliency to endure a long financial drought? Can those entrepreneurs who must rebuild or repair their businesses identify funding sources to take on such expense? At the time of this writing, these are, at least partially, unanswered questions.

Largely, it does seem that times are changing, so hope remains. Certainly, CDFIs like CRF will be present to help fund such enterprise. The more vexing question is can these institutions do so at the scale required to create meaningful and sustainable change? We might take heart in the corporate response to these events that aspects of capitalism are changing with the times. As mentioned earlier the Paycheck Protection Program provided direct relief to end users like small-business owners in ways the 2008 safety nets chose not to. Companies like Goldman Sachs and Bank of America leaned in to the challenge and opportunity the COVID-19 pandemic presented to the tune of hundreds of millions of dollars that enabled organizations like CRF to work with the smallest businesses most at risk of failing. In another example, in the immediate wake of George Floyd's murder, Minneapolis-headquartered Target pledged $10 million to social justice organizations such as the National Urban League and the African American Leadership Forum. It promised to spend $2 billion with Black-owned businesses by 2025. Target also committed to provide ten thousand hours of pro bono consulting services for businesses owned by people of color within the Twin Cities. For Target's own properties requiring repair in the wake of civil unrest, it wasted no time or capital investment, and its Lake Street store, closest in proximity among its holdings to the site of Floyd's murder, reopened with a rebranded approach that better reflects its neighborhood and carries more products specific to the needs of its neighbors. U.S. Bank, also headquartered in Minneapolis, swiftly changed its corporate giving and investing programs to respond to the events, and countless other companies joined their ranks to respond to the cries for systemic change.

In the weeks following Floyd's murder, American corporations pledged $50 billion toward racial equity. Whether their pledges will actually materialize will provide us real insight into whether this trend toward support of social enterprises is authentic. A lot remains to be seen regarding the rebuilding of tangible assets, not to mention intangible assets like trust. This takes decades, whereas their destruction can occur in a moment. Sadly, the early evidence is mixed. Some entities risk returning either to the patterns of mostly unconscious systemic bias or public affairs campaigns that are not matched by action. A May 2021 study by Creative Investment Research offered analysis that only $250 million has actually been spent or committed to specific initiatives. Among the exceptions have been Target, Apple, U.S. Bank, and MasterCard through its Center for Inclusive Growth, which have pledged millions of dollars to serve predominantly BIPOC-owned small businesses over the coming years. We can't know yet if other major corporations will use the tools of capitalism to meaningfully address problems, as Apple did with the first round of its multi-million-dollar commitment by donating $25 million to Propel Center, a learning hub for historically Black colleges and universities.[25] An optimist by nature, I remain hopeful.

Personally, I believe the clearest path to sustainable change is for corporations to partner with social enterprises like CDFIs that have expertise in applying the tools of finance. What I know for certain is that a successful rebound in Minneapolis and elsewhere will require more than resiliency of spirit; it will demand capital reinvestment, and reinvestment requires investors who believe there is value in putting money to work for the good of others and the collective community even if they understandably also wish to see financial returns on their investment.

MOVING TOWARD AN INCLUSIVE VISION OF CAPITALISM

If corporations will support the Business Roundtable statement mentioned above with real action, it most certainly will be a shift from the belief system acted upon by most throughout the years CRF has been in business. Despite the historical presence of public/private systems I have introduced, most of the American vision of capitalism that has thrived aligns with Milton Friedman's philosophy that extolled the virtues of a free-market economic system with minimal government intervention in social matters. That dominant model is built on the assumption that a corporation's only objective is to maximize profits for its shareholders. Friedman, a Nobel Prize winner for economics, had his heyday as an advisor to President Ronald Reagan, when he contributed to a free-market belief in trickle-down economics that the money from tax breaks and benefits for corpora-

---

25   Marco Quiroz-Gutierrez, "American Companies Pledged $50 Billion to Black Communities. Most of It Hasn't Materialized," *Fortune*, May 6, 2021, https://fortune.com/2021/05/06/us-companies-black-communities-money-50-billion/.

tions and the wealthy will flow through a market, eventually reach everyone else, and stimulate growth. Empirical evidence continues to suggest that the theory never achieved its stated goals. What we saw instead over the last fifty years is such an approach to capitalism that creates private benefits and public costs, the condition I have already identified through the economic term of negative externalities. It also has led to a widening wealth gap—especially among people of color—that threatens the very stability of our society. The sorts of small-business owners operating in most communities of color certainly did not see a trickle-down effect in Reagan's era and still await this promised benefit waterfall.

The dedication American capitalism has held toward Friedman's principles has been the dominant force for decades, but as the Business Roundtable statement suggests, we may have reached an age when such devotion is ending. I'd like to think that one element of this change has been the rise of innovative investment tools like those developed by CRF and other CDFIs. Building on a belief that capitalism has to be harnessed for the good of all, the financial institutions in the social enterprise space have proven that the right kind of investment can make a difference. While even collectively our industry has made only modest investments when compared to the entirety of the market, at CRF we have been successful in bringing virtually every major U.S. bank in as investment partners alongside major insurance companies, pension funds, and private investors. The success of public, private, and nonprofit partnerships that invited capital investment in small businesses, housing ownership, and other community development has proven a capital markets concept can work. The people we have had the tremendous opportunity to serve in turn demonstrate that businesses and the communities in which they are located can thrive when provided opportunity.

Have we reached a point of critical mass sufficient to constitute a trend? Not yet, but we definitely have a road map. More importantly still, those entities we have funded prove that investment can accomplish impact that goes beyond individuals. We have witnessed how de-risking investments in order to leverage much greater amounts of private capital can help entrepreneurs harness impact that then radiates into a larger community and foments a sense of pride. Change starts when we believe the measure of capitalism's success isn't only demonstrated by a number on a balance sheet or the size of a shareholder dividend.

Since I entered the social enterprise space in the 1980s, the drivers behind such initiatives haven't changed, but where I entered the arena of social entrepreneurship when it was in a nascent stage, today there are not only sophisticated mechanisms for promoting social ventures; it has also become an established principle. The concepts of social enterprise investment are now taught in the premier business schools throughout the world, including Oxford, Harvard, Yale, Stanford, Penn, Brown, and New York University, their presence a testimony to the recognition that the economy of the near future will depart in critical ways from the economy of the past half century. In the Columbia University School of Business's new building, its architects developed a design that "reflects the close fit of the architecture to person-to-person connection and intensified interaction—what the school's leadership sees as essential to the sprawling aspirations it has for its graduates to do good as they make money."[26] Most of the world's largest banks now have dedicated departments for responsible investing. The legal and regulatory environment is changing to

---

26   James S. Russell, "At Columbia's $600 Million Business School, Time to Rethink Capitalism," *New York Times*, January 5, 2023, https://www.nytimes.com/2023/01/05/arts/design/columbia-business-school-diller-scofidio-renfro-kravis-geffen.html.

reinforce and permit social enterprises, particularly with the formal recognition in corporate law of public benefit corporations that explicitly permit a company to be created for a public benefit beyond profit maximization. Public benefit corporations are for-profit entities authorized by thirty-five U.S. states and the District of Columbia that include positive impact on society, workers, the community, and the environment in addition to profit as their legally defined goals. Most notable among these is Delaware, which is the state of choice by many for incorporation; when Delaware passed its law, it was a signal to markets nationwide that benefit corporations were for real. Benefit corporations are vehicles of modern social ventures that are not simply created for the benefit of the shareholders or the owners but that take the interests of other stakeholders into account as part of their purpose. The movement toward formal declaration as a public benefit corporation by companies is typically a mix of genuinely wanting to help solve problems, a growing recognition that a corporation has larger responsibilities to the social good, a desire to gain community recognition for its values, and a modern understanding that companies can realize sustainable profits without having profit become the singular motive for their existence. In many ways such companies increasingly reflect the make-up of their workforce, where more and more employees, particularly educated, white-collar workers, see value in working for enterprises that demonstrate tangible inclusive, open-minded cultures that are mission driven. Setting aside the Supreme Court's Citizens United ruling that companies are people, companies increasingly mirror the broader society, where new estimates show that nearly four out of ten Americans identify with a race or ethnic group other than White.[27]

It is now common for corporate rating agencies to produce what are labeled ESG scores, an evaluation of a company's environmental and social impact and its governance structure. Typically, a score is compiled from data collected surrounding specific metrics related to intangible assets within the enterprise. They can be considered a form of corporate social credit scores. More and more ESG scores are factored in when calculating a company's future enterprise value because there is increasing pressure to measure the sustainability and societal impact of a company. This trend is now entrenched enough that it has drawn scrutiny, as the West Virginia action demonstrates.

Measurements of a company's sustainability and environmental impact include metrics like its carbon footprint through monitoring of its carbon emissions or its use of or production of recyclable products. There is a great deal of scientific data available that provide tangible measurements of environmental impact. Because more and more consumers now make purchasing decisions based on such factors, investors have taken notice. They have also become more long term in their approach to investments and consider a company's dependency on fossil fuels and therefore its contributions to global climate change as part of their assessment of its value and its long-term cost structure. Similarly, investors now regularly factor in a company's contribution to the depletion of resources or future obsolescence of a company's product or service.

Measurements of social factors in ESG are more difficult to quantify with empirical data, for often it is difficult to detangle the

27   William Frey, "The Nation Is Diversifying Even Faster Than Predicted, According to New Census Data," Brookings Institute, July 1, 2020, https://www.brookings.edu/research/new-census-data-shows-the-nation-is-diversifying-even-faster-than-predicted/.

full scale of economic impacts of ventures associated with things like the larger contribution to a community's overall economy from cooperative investment in a new manufacturing facility or the ripple effects of greater homeownership. Often it comes down to trying to pin down causality versus correlation. Some hard data do exist, and there is typically ample anecdotal evidence, though measuring the impact of investment in social programs like affordable housing can be as much art as science. If we are able to create a mechanism for funding expansion of a small manufacturing business in a historically underfinanced community of color, we have ample hard data points to measure the growth of the business, the growth in numbers of employees, perhaps even how and where those employees spend their money; we can know if more employees are able to afford homes in the community, or track the number of minority-owned suppliers the business partners with, but what is far harder to know is if the success of this business sparks the arrival of other new businesses or if a decline in violent crime rates in the community has connection to the availability of new jobs or greater stability among workers. Over my career I have witnessed investment in diverse entrepreneurs establish positive change in communities with a ripple effect, though I do not always have volumes of statistical data to support the effects I have seen.

What we can know for certain is that the larger population of the U.S. is value aligned with ESG principles, a trend that has taken a strong hold. As with environmentally conscious investing, when it comes to social issues, investors increasingly reflect larger socially minded values expressed by consumers and by shareholders. *Harvard Business Review* brings home this clear trend:

> According to the ESG research and advisory firm Institutional Shareholder Services, 476 environmental and social

(E&S) shareholder resolutions had been filed in the United States as of August 10, 2018. The share of total resolutions focused on E&S has grown from around 33% in the 2006 to 2010 time period to around 45% from 2011 to 2016. By 2017, it stood at just over 50%.[28]

Investors hold *the* powerful tool for fueling such change. And executives are taking note. After reporters from *Harvard Business Review* interviewed seventy senior executives at forty-three global institutional investing firms, they discovered that ESG was almost universally top of mind for these executives.[29]

Measuring corporate governance structures is relatively easy; changing the make-up of those structures is difficult and time consuming, but again we live in a time when consumers and investors are demanding change. Scrutiny of board make-up and diversity in senior leadership teams is now common. More and more investors pay attention to corporate behavior practices, board diversity, executive pay, ownership, and accounting practices, including things like the balance of power between CEOs and board chairpersons and the nature of executive compensation packages. More potential employees evaluate a company based on workplace culture and assessment reports, and companies have responded by vying for placement on "best company to work for" lists, recognizing they must compete for the best talent. Employees and investors increasingly demand fairness and gender and racial equity in compensation. Generally, there is now a common perception that a company's workforce and its board make-up reflect its stakeholders. Corporate America is far, far behind in fulfilling this

---

28   Robert G. Eccles and Svetlana Klimenko, "The Investor Revolution: Shareholders Are Getting Serious about Sustainability," *Harvard Business Review*, May-June 2019, https://hbr.org/2019/05/the-investor-revolution.

29   Eccles and Klimenko, "Investor Revolution."

reflection, but there is little tolerance for the status quo beyond, and often among, the wealthy elites who have long been the primary beneficiaries of a purely shareholder-driven profit motivation. Investors need to take notice. There's a very real cultural shift occurring that has entropy. Those shouting in protest after yet another murder of a Black man in police custody are not voices in isolation, and they are not going away. Mindful investors have joined the chorus. The faces we have come to expect to be seated at boardroom tables are changing. To insist on sustaining such change is not only a moral perspective but is also the factual reality of a multicultural society founded on protecting the rights of all its citizens.

Cumulatively, all three concerns—environmental, social, and governance—factor into ESG scores. I place all three as elemental to a full understanding of impact investing and critical to the future of business success. It's true that the broad outlines I've offered here in environmental, social, and corporate governance concerns ask for an ethical investment portfolio—my own original and foundational interest in the world of impact investing sprung from a moral view of a need to promote change and solve social problems—the work, the opportunity, and the need behind it step beyond ethics to contemporary practicalities. We live in an age when it is not just high time we focus on the impacts of all stakeholders because it's the right thing to do; it's necessary for a stable society and a just economy. Evidence suggests that companies with sustainable business practices demonstrate increased profitability

> WE LIVE IN AN AGE WHEN IT IS NOT JUST HIGH TIME WE FOCUS ON THE IMPACTS OF ALL STAKEHOLDERS BECAUSE IT'S THE RIGHT THING TO DO; IT'S NECESSARY FOR A STABLE SOCIETY AND A JUST ECONOMY.

and higher valuations. A 2020 study from Institutional Shareholder Services found that a direct link exists between a company's ESG performance and its financial performance.[30] In 2020, "three out of four sustainable equity funds outperformed their Morningstar averages while the majority of ESG equity index funds beat conventional index funds, even when accounting for their comparatively higher operating costs."[31] In his 2020 and 2021 annual letters to CEOs, Larry Fink, CEO of BlackRock, the world's largest investment manager, emphasized corporate and environmental responsibility and noted that beyond just shareholder value, corporate behavior will drive his firm's investment decision-making. In 2021 the U.S. Securities and Exchange Commission proposed enhancing the rules that require corporate disclosures of ESG-related activities as part of its annual regulatory agenda. I would add that, against common misperception, social entrepreneurship doesn't mean taking away from the opportunity for one to make money from investment by giving that money to another; it is an act of investment in both the great American experiment of democracy and the American belief in capitalism.

Was CRF a trendsetter? Perhaps. Certainly, we were players in social enterprise experiments from a time in which only a few people around the country might be able to define what they were. The atmosphere has changed dramatically since the beginning years of CRF. Yet, in many ways, the battle to elevate economic opportunity for all remains a fledgling field. Keeping that in mind, let me next address, in more precise terms, exactly what I mean by social enterprise and why it can be so transformative.

---

30   Kevin Spellman, "ESG Matters," Institutional Shareholder Services, January 9, 2020, https://www.issgovernance.com/library/esg-matters/.

31   Rebecca Baldridge, "Sustainable ESG Investing Isn't Just the Right Thing to Do, It's Now Paying Real Financial Dividends," *Robb Report*, June 14, 2021, https://robbreport.com/lifestyle/finance/esg-investing-1234618185/.

CHAPTER 4

WHAT IS A SOCIAL ENTERPRISE?

In order to understand better the trends shaping the current era and the tools available to create change, we first need to define some terms.

Just what is a social enterprise? What role do social ventures play in the financial marketplace and to shape the future of investing? Bill Drayton, the founder of the social enterprise philanthropic organization Ashoka, is widely credited with coining the term "social entrepreneurship" in the 1980s. Jill Kickul and Thomas Lyons, the authors of *Understanding Social Entrepreneurship*, point out in attempting to define the "social" portion of social entrepreneurship that it "has to do with anything that pertains to a community or society. By definition, it puts society ahead of the individual."[32] They go on to point out that people have a tendency to think that the social aspect of life is distinct from the economic, a viewpoint that has helped U.S.-based capitalism embrace a belief that the government should keep

---

32   Jill Kickul and Thomas S. Lyons, *Understanding Social Entrepreneurship: The Relentless Pursuit of Mission in an Ever Changing World* (New York: Routledge, 2012), 13.

its hands off private economic pursuits (laissez-faire) and that it is society's responsibility to protect itself from unscrupulous business practices (caveat emptor). Kickul and Lyons suggest that defining "social entrepreneurship," then, is trickier still, for not only is it a concept that continues to change and grow and many niche experts have different visions, but they broadly suggest that a social entrepreneur is an "innovator who adds value to people's lives by pursuing a social mission, using the processes, tools, and techniques of business entrepreneurship."[33] Whether for-profit, nonprofit, public, or a hybrid of the three, the social entrepreneur puts societal benefit ahead of his or her personal gain and uses any "profits" realized to expand the reach of his or her mission.

Let me add to their definition by sharing a story of social entrepreneurship in action. From 1994 until 2004, an enormous sixteen-story art deco building formerly owned by the Sears Company sat vacant, its glory faded, sections of it exposed to the harsh Minneapolis winters. Its slow deterioration was repeated in many of the businesses and homes of the surrounding neighborhoods. The original part of the building bordering Elliot Avenue and Lake Street in Midtown dated back to 1928. The building underwent numerous expansions, until it ballooned to 1.2 million square feet, much of its massive space devoted to a warehouse in addition to a flagship department store and office space. We all know the story of Sears, a company once synonymous with American retail, now reduced to a shadow of its former self and struggling to emerge from its 2018 bankruptcy filing. Vacant and in disrepair, the building was seen by some as an eyesore. Others saw in it an opportunity. These competing perspectives often extended to the surrounding neighborhoods of south Minneapolis,

---

33   Kickul and Lyons, *Understanding Social Entrepreneurship*, 14.

which had increasingly become home to populations of immigrants and their decedents, especially those arriving from Latin America and Somalia. The building is located in the Phillips neighborhood, one of the poorest in the city and one of the most ethnically diverse census tracts in the country.

After numerous failed development proposals, the city of Minneapolis acquired the site in 2001. Neighbors and local business owners helped convince city officials that the historical building should be saved and reimagined to reflect the ethnic diversity of the neighborhood and the entrepreneurial energy of the businesses on Lake Street. Neighborhood Development Center, Latino Economic Development Center, CRF, and other organizations were working with small businesses on Lake Street to fill empty storefronts by providing training and loans.

In 2004 much of the building was redeveloped as the Midtown Exchange, a mix of apartments, retail, and office space, including the corporate headquarters of Allina Health. The redevelopment project includes the Midtown Global Market, which occupies the former Sears retail store and is home to a variety of small, independently owned restaurants, cafés, and specialty grocers. The market hosts community programs including music, dance, and children's activities. The Midtown Exchange and the Midtown Global Market took shape through the extraordinary efforts of a wide range of people: entrepreneurs, three CDFIs, other community organizations, local corporations, the city of Minneapolis, countless donors, lenders, and tax credit investors. Working together they made this rebirth of decaying infrastructure a success. The small businesses that make up Midtown Global Market offer a rich example of what can occur through public, private, and nonprofit alliances. Opening for business in 2006, eighteen of the original businesses are still present. They have contributed to making Midtown Global Market a vibrant economic and cultural center where the community gathers. It's now home to forty-five businesses spanning twenty-two cultures and provides a global experience to its visitors with an extraordinary variety of tastes, art, and crafts. In 2018 over 1.5 million patrons visited Midtown Global Market.

By nature and design, social enterprises involve stakeholders far beyond the "owners." As I noted when I turned to definitions of the term "social entrepreneurship," social enterprises can be financial investment by nonprofit entities or by for-profit companies, including those that are public benefit corporations that have explicit requirements for creating a benefit to those beyond their owners. The expansive vision of a project like the Midtown Exchange is illustrative of a trend in capitalism and an explicit safe harbor against the Milton Friedman dictum. Social enterprises are often initiated by CDFIs, community coalitions, and community foundations, particularly those focused on providing financial services to low-income communities. Many of the foundations and nonprofit organizations that germinate the grassroots for larger social enterprise investment are the definition of philanthropy that Milton Friedman suggested had no meaningful role in a marketplace. These kinds of social enterprises offer a counterbalance to financial markets that have, time and again, failed to solve pressing social problems.

Social enterprises take on all sorts of problems and take on different forms. Close to home and personally meaningful to me is the social enterprise developed by my daughter, Miriam Altman, who is the cofounder and CEO of Kinvolved, which is focused on the vexing problem of student absenteeism. Drawing on her experience as a high school history teacher in New York City, Miriam found that the most successful intervention for chronic student absenteeism was to build a strong, two-way relationship with students and their families. After seeing success in combating the problem through work with a faculty strategy team, Miriam wondered if it were possible to scale the solutions they had applied and to bring in technology as a tool. Combining software she and her partners developed with research-based human interventions, they set about changing the deeply ingrained behaviors and external factors affecting student attendance, including poverty, racism, and socioeconomic exclusion. This mix of applied technology that enhanced communication among schools, families, and students and offered professional services to teachers and administrators offered tremendous results, including a 22 percent reduction in absenteeism among English-language learners and an 11 percent improvement in graduation rates. In 2022 Kinvolved, a public benefit corporation, sold to PowerSchool, a publicly traded company, in order to further scale its reach. Kinvolved is an excellent example of applying innovative tools to battle chronic, systemic problems. Just as PowerSchool recognized the potency of original thinking and the robust infrastructure Kinvolved had developed as an approach that could be applied in school districts all over the country, I am confident that the financial world has evolved to a point where it understands the pressing need to embrace the approaches and philosophies developed by CRF and other CDFIs and move the products and services they offer from the margins to the mainstream. Capital markets are now poised to demand that for-profit entities become social minded.

Social enterprises can be an extremely effective means of creating multistakeholder solutions to what have been entrenched problems. Their kryptonite: applying their abilities at sufficient scale. Entrenched challenges need specialized solutions that can rarely be extrapolated to many other entrenched challenges. Scale is not limited by the problems social enterprises set out to solve, but by the resources and efforts necessary for each unique solution. In a financial sense, the primary mechanism for trying to meet that challenge the best we can arrives in an understanding of risk that is distinct from most traditional financial institutions, as we will explore next.

CHAPTER 5

TAKING THE RISKS BANKS WON'T

In the financial industry, when considering investments and loans, there is a constant evaluation of perceived risk. Similar to how public health administrators try to predict the spread of potential contagions through practical analysis of sources of risk and opportunities for spread, bankers try to assess the likelihood that a loan or investment will produce a return as efficiently as possible. Much of investing hinges on trying to find a balance point between manageable risk and maximum profit. Financial risk management is the process of identification, analysis, and mitigation of uncertainty in investment decisions. But risk is, as the saying goes, inseparable from return.

FINANCIAL RISK MANAGEMENT STRATEGY

Part of the problem when it comes to creating equitable access to capital is that risk management processes have been set up for expediency. We have created a system that is aimed at efficiently making lending decisions, one that necessarily relies heavily on data, particularly on credit scores. Businesses use automated quantification of consumer credit histories in the form of credit scores to make objective decisions about when to extend credit and on what terms. In the current era, when traditional banks must compete with more loosely regulated fintech companies, there is even greater desire to automate and make credit decisions faster. Whether applying for a credit card, a consumer loan, a mortgage, or an insurance policy, credit scores typically determine access to credit. Some employers even use credit scores to make employment decisions. In theory this all sounds fine. But in practice, in the name of efficiency, many people are excluded by such a system. Historically, Black, Latino, and Native American people have had asymmetrical access to the mechanisms that elevate credit scores and to financial services generally. In a bit of a catch-22, in order to develop a credit score, one must utilize credit. And that means, for starters, those seeking credit must have an established relationship with a bank or credit union. What if they don't?

> **HISTORICALLY, BLACK, LATINO, AND NATIVE AMERICAN PEOPLE HAVE HAD ASYMMETRICAL ACCESS TO THE MECHANISMS THAT ELEVATE CREDIT SCORES AND TO FINANCIAL SERVICES GENERALLY.**

According to the 2017 FDIC Survey of Unbanked and Underbanked Households, "one in four households (25.2 percent)" was "unbanked or underbanked, conducting some or all of their financial transactions outside of the mainstream banking system," relying on alternative financial services providers, cash, or other financial arrangements.[34] The term "underbanked" refers to those who have a bank account but rely on alternative financial services such as money orders, check-cashing services, and payday loans rather than on traditional loans and credit cards to manage their finances and fund purchases. Lower-income, Black and Hispanic, working-age disabled, and foreign-born, noncitizen households were more likely to have had no mainstream credit. These differences persist even after accounting for other socioeconomic and demographic characteristics (such as income, education, and age) and bank account ownership. Making up just 32 percent of the U.S. population, Black and Hispanic households represent 64 percent of the country's unbanked and 47 percent of its underbanked households.[35] Almost 17 percent of Black households and 14 percent of Hispanic households were unbanked in 2017.[36] These rates reflect a significant improvement from the 2009 survey, mostly accounted for by an overall economic improvement nationwide, yet bank account ownership among Black and Hispanic households continues to remain significantly below the national average, and while we do not have comprehensive data available yet, the COVID-related recession of 2020 will undoubtedly create more un- and underbanked households among minorities and stagnate their ability to access credit.

In many ways the challenges associated with underbanked communities is an old one. But there are ways in which it's a new one as well. Without taking a position on the harms or benefits of a cashless society, it does appear clear that commerce is moving away from cash

---

34 Federal Deposit Insurance Corporation, "2017 FDIC National Survey of Unbanked and Under-banked Households," December 17, 2017, https://www.fdic.gov/analysis/household-survey/2017/index.html.

35 Kedra Newsom Reeves et al., "Racial Equity in Banking Starts with Busting the Myths," Boston Capital Group, February 2, 2021, https://www.bcg.com/publications/2021/unbanked-and-under-banked-households-breaking-down-the-myths-towards-racial-equity-in-banking.

36 Reeves et al., "Racial Equity."

transactions at a breathtaking pace. On the consumer side, what does it mean to underbanked communities when restaurants or hair salons will only accept card payments? On the business side, too, neighborhood stores may miss out on sales because of limited ability to accept payment via cards and new technology.

Part of the reason for the underbanking of Black and Latino communities is that check cashers and payday lenders are more common than bank branches. There are some rational reasons for this. Payday lenders are more likely to be open beyond the traditional "banker's hours," something important for those who work outside traditional business hours. In some communities, there simply are no bank branches present. Payday-style lenders generally charge exorbitant interest rates and apply other transaction fees, far higher than those charged by banks. In general, however, these costs and fees are clearly posted, and the borrower has easy-to-understand repayment responsibilities. In the short run, such lenders can help people cope with income volatility and allow them to avoid the wait times involved for mainstream financial institutions to clear transactions. In the long run, however, these loans can become a trap that leads to a vicious cycle of high interest, late fees, and other costs that can choke the borrower.

Black and Hispanic adults in the United States remain less likely than White adults to own a computer or have high-speed internet at home, making it difficult to manage many of the processes affiliated with loans, mortgages, and required business transactions through online banking systems.[37] Banking apps on mobile devices show some promise for opening greater access to those who might otherwise

---

37   Sara Atske and Andrew Perrin, "Home Broadband Adoption, Computer Ownership Vary by Race, Ethnicity in the U.S.," Pew Research Center, July 16, 2021, https://www.pewresearch.org/fact-tank/2021/07/16/home-broadband-adoption-computer-ownership-vary-by-race-ethnicity-in-the-u-s/.

remain unbanked and also offer a partial explanation for increasing interest in fintech products. These sorts of developments in financial institutions may prove critical for the future of those who typically have either eschewed banks or have been excluded, for without bank accounts, consumers cannot generate the data that help establish creditworthiness.

The consequences of not establishing credit are real. Look no further than the tragic results from businesses that could not seek assistance through the Paycheck Protection Program (PPP). Banks generally made loans to businesses that had significant banking relationships including checking accounts and outstanding loans. Sole proprietors without significant banking relationships were often unable to access PPP loans from their banks. The loss of small community banks, predominantly in communities of color, was another important contributing factor in racial disparities that emerged, particularly in the early stages of the PPP program. As reported by the Institute for Local Self-Reliance,

> Recent surveys have found that businesses owned by people of color have been much less likely to secure one of these relief loans. A long-standing pattern of discrimination in bank lending is one reason. Another reason may be that communities of color have fewer local banks. In research not yet published, we found that counties with a higher share of African American residents have lost nearly half of their small community banks since 2006. This is a significantly steeper decline in local banks than other counties experienced.[38]

---

38 Stacy Mitchell, "Update: PPP Loan Data Continues to Show That Big Bank Consolidation Has Hampered Small Business Relief," Institute for Local Self-Reliance, June 15, 2020, https://ilsr.org/update-ppp-loan-data/.

The inequity present in the PPP program mirrors long-standing patterns that reveal how larger shifts in market patterns and historical dependency on processes established by large banks can impact people's financial lives. The unbanked and underbanked have a difficult time purchasing homes, investing in education, or funding a business venture.

The nature of how most financial decisions regarding credit are made may not be racist by intent, but the system we have created is an inherently inequitable one, and the features that make it inequitable are deeply tangled within its history and its policies. What is clear are the results, which made for startling headlines in 2022, when Wells Fargo, the nation's largest mortgage provider, approved only 47 percent of Black homeowners who completed a refinance application.[39] The bank explained the low approval rate by stating that it treats all potential borrowers the same and is more selective than other lenders. An internal review of the bank's 2020 refinancing decisions confirmed that "additional, legitimate, credit-related factors" were responsible for the differences.[40]

We don't have to search any further than redlining policies to understand what systemic racism looks like. Racial discrimination in organizational practices and structures arises within institutions, for institutions by their very nature are not immune from inheriting or perpetuating attitudes, policies, or practices reflective of racial assumptions or prejudice. Blatant or unintentional, the effect remains the same.

As with all aspects of systemic racism, untangling the policies that have emerged over time is difficult and complex because differential

---

39 Shawn Donnan et al., "Wells Fargo Rejected Half Its Black Applicants in Mortgage Refinancing Boom," Bloomberg, March 10, 2022, https://www.bloomberg.com/graphics/2022-wells-fargo-black-home-loan-refinancing/.

40 Donnan et al., "Wells Fargo Rejected."

treatment based on race, gender, and ancestry is deeply entrenched in many elements of the larger socioeconomic system. Often, hidden bias emerges out of entrenched systemic policies because assumption or negative stereotypes form from established worldviews. If worldviews are narrow because people are exposed to limited diversity in their daily lives, and if they are reinforced by social groups—both in actual life and on social media—such worldviews can impact decision-making, including high-stakes decisions about who does and who does not receive credit.

While hidden or unconscious biases are not unique to large-scale financial institutions, the bigger the corporation, the more likely there is greater bureaucracy and uniform policy involved in analyzing creditworthiness.

RISK AND THE RACIAL WEALTH GAP

The difficulties experienced by the unbanked, underbanked, and those who have had limited access to credit are exacerbated by the larger racial wealth divide that is a central feature of the current U.S. capital market.

According to the Federal Reserve, the net worth of a typical White family is $171,000, *ten* times greater than that of a Black family.[41] As the Association for Enterprise Opportunity detailed in its report "The Tapestry of Black Business Ownership in America,"

> This wealth gap is perpetuated by a cycle of little to no inter-
> generational wealth transfer among Black Americans to their
> children, especially U.S.-born Blacks. Consequently, home
> ownership and other asset-building activities are suppressed,

---

41   Kriston McIntosh et al., "Examining the Black-White Wealth Gap," Brookings, February 27, 2020,
       https://www.brookings.edu/blog/up-front/2020/02/27/examining-the-black-white-wealth-gap/.

the ability to locate into higher-quality school systems is thwarted, and fewer people receive postsecondary educations. Limited credentials in turn narrow work opportunities and result in high unemployment figures relative to the rest of the country.[42]

Three-generation poverty (literally poverty that extends across three generations of a family) is over sixteen times higher among Black adults than White adults (21.3 percent and 1.2 percent, respectively). In other words one in five Black Americans is experiencing poverty for the third generation in a row, compared to just one in a hundred White Americans.[43]

Circumstances *are* changing, sometimes for the better and sometimes for the worse. For example, the national (overall) poverty rate fell from 15.1 percent in 2010 to 11.4 percent in 2020, with the most sizable decline among Black and Hispanic Americans. And since 1990 middle-class wealth increased 82.1 percent. *However*, this substantial middle-class increase in wealth carries an important caveat, for over that period middle-class families moved from owning 12.2 percent of total U.S. wealth in 1990 to just 7.2 percent in 2021. Over that same period, the wealth of the top 1 percent increased by 379.9 percent.[44] Some additional economic facts should prove instructive on the nature of the widening wealth gap. Consider the following data:

- A *Washington Post* article from January of 2022 focused on the gains that the richest Americans made during the COVID-19

---

42   Association for Enterprise Opportunity, "The Tapestry of Black Business Ownership in America: Untapped Opportunities for Success," https://aeoworks.org/wp-content/uploads/2019/03/AEO_Black_Owned_Business_Report_02_16_17_FOR_WEB-1.pdf.

43   Scott Winship et al., "Long Shadows: The Black-White Gap in Multigenerational Poverty," Brookings Institute, June 10, 2021, https://www.brookings.edu/research/long-shadows-the-black-white-gap-in-multigenerational-poverty/.

44   USA Facts, "How Has the American Standard of Living Changed? How Does the Government Help the Disadvantaged?" https://usafacts.org/state-of-the-union/standard-living/.

pandemic, stating that 2021 was "the best time in history to be one of America's 745 billionaires, whose cumulative wealth has grown by an estimated 70 percent since the beginning of the pandemic even as tens of millions of low-wage workers have lost their jobs or their homes. Together, those 745 billionaires are now worth more than the bottom 60 percent of American households combined."[45]

• According to a paper by economist Edward N. Wolff in 2017, the wealthiest 1 percent of American households owned 40 percent of the country's wealth, a share higher than at any point since 1962. Wolff drew his data from the federal Survey of Consumer Finances. In the five years from 2013 to 2017, the share of wealth owned by the wealthiest 1 percent shot up by nearly 3 percentage points. Wealth owned by the bottom 90 percent fell over the same period.[46]

The history of the United States is linked inextricably with a national vision of itself as a place where anyone can thrive. While wealth creation is all part of the charm of the American dream, and while there remains the prospect of "pulling oneself up by one's bootstraps" so commonly present in American consciousness, when placed in an international context, the United States has not collectively thrived when it comes to realizing income distribution. Consider where it stands on the Gini coefficient, the most commonly used measure of income distribution. The higher the Gini coefficient, the greater the gap between the incomes of a country's richest and poorest

45   Eli Saslow, "The Moral Calculations of a Billionaire," washingtonpost.com (WP Company, December 7, 2022), https://www.washingtonpost.com/nation/2022/01/30/moral-calculations-billionaire/.

46   Christopher Ingraham, "The Richest 1 Percent Now Owns More of the Country's Wealth Than at Any Time in the Past 50 Years," *Washington Post*, December 6, 2017, https://www.washingtonpost.com/news/wonk/wp/2017/12/06/the-richest-1-percent-now-owns-more-of-the-countrys-wealth-than-at-any-time-in-the-past-50-years/.

people. Based on the most recent World Bank data from 2018, the United States had a Gini coefficient of 41.4.[47] That places the U.S. almost level with countries like Peru and Bolivia on this metric, and few would turn to much of Latin America as the hallmark of wealth distribution.

The degree of influence exerted by the wealthiest 1 percent is a harder thing to measure. But it is fair to make some assumptions in a political climate that has made lobbying a fine art and allowed a handful of rich donors to dominate the backing of political candidates (particularly in the wake of the Citizens United decision, which reversed century-old campaign finance restrictions and enabled corporations and other outside groups to spend unlimited funds on elections). We might do well to recall that in 2016 the U.S. elected a billionaire to the presidency in a race that featured multiple billionaire candidates and that there are, at the time of this writing, at least three governorships held by billionaires. Given the number of multimillionaires serving in Congress, I am probably not stretching an assumption that wealth can convey influence, as a comprehensive examination of political campaign donations could illuminate were it not for the obfuscation provided by the various PACs, committees, and corporate and lobbying organizations.

THE INVESTMENT CONTINUUM

If we are to change the dynamics of institutional racism in lending, it is necessary to create a new risk/reward paradigm that incorporates social returns as well as financial returns. It is essential that we interro-

47   World Population Review, "Gini Coefficient by Country 2022," https://worldpopulationreview.com/country-rankings/gini-coefficient-by-country.

gate the financial products, processes, and policies that systematically deny access to credit—particularly to people of color.

Systemic discrimination requires systemic remedies. That means we have to understand more about how the financial credit system works. To better understand why many have been underserved by financial institutions, we must understand how risk is perceived and managed by them. Any number of experienced individuals in the CDFI world in particular and among other financial professionals and economists regularly speak about the continuum of risk, but among them I hold particularly high regard for the work of Luther Ragin Jr. and his discussions of risk management in funding social ventures. He is the retired president and founding CEO of the Global Impact Investing Network (GIIN). Prior to joining the GIIN, he served as vice president for investments at FB Heron Foundation for ten years, where he oversaw its $300 million endowment, steadily increasing the impact investing allocation to more than 40 percent, while maintaining competitive, risk-adjusted total financial returns. CRF has been lucky to have Luther serve as one of our board members and has benefited from his counsel. The graphic below captures Ragin's visualization for a continuum of risk:

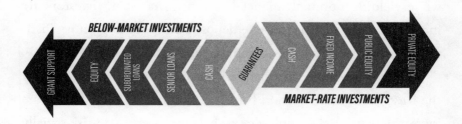

This model represents the dichotomy of maximizing financial risk and return on the right end of the continuum, while maximizing social return and risk on the left side. Let me elaborate. Private equity investments generally have the highest risk among financial investments. They are generally illiquid and face business operational risk and many other factors that may lead to subpar returns or downright financial losses—hence the high risk. At the same time, the opportunity for large upsides in the few investments that take off can lead to exceedingly large financial returns. Market-rate investors tend to ignore social returns in making investment decisions while seeking to maximize financial returns, but, when properly structured, market-rate investments can generate targeted social returns as well.

As we move from the right end of the continuum toward the center, investments take on less risk and less return. Equity investments in public companies are generally lower risk than private companies: they are liquid and valued daily on exchanges. Here, too, investors may take social returns into account. ESG considerations increasingly influence investment decisions seeking to minimize climate change or maximize investments in emerging clean technologies.

Market-rate fixed-income investments have even lower risk/reward characteristics. CRF has issued millions of dollars in fixed-income community reinvestment notes over the years that generate market-rate risk-adjusted returns while also seeking social returns.

Cash, in the form of insured deposits, is the safest investment, while yielding nominal financial returns. That said, investors are increasingly making market-rate deposits in CDFI depository institutions to enable them to accomplish their social missions.

Guarantees may either be market rate or below market. Led by the Kresge, Rockefeller, and FB Heron foundations, foundations are increasingly using their unleveraged balance sheets to de-risk socially impactful investments through guarantees.

Turning to the other end of the continuum, charitable contributions or grants are among the highest-risk transactions in that they solely seek social returns. When a donor makes a grant, the donor is taking a risk that the expected social return may not materialize. Once the money is gone, it cannot be recovered. Grant makers have become increasingly diligent at evaluating outcomes data in determining where to make their donations.

For the purposes of this book, we are specifically interested in mission-related investments because they are made by mission-based organizations, such as foundations that are developing social ventures. The potential for financial return is a key characteristic often used to distinguish the range of investments a foundation or social investor may make.

As a result most nonprofit organizations see foundations as only a source of grants. But foundations have another important and lesser-known tool for helping organizations with a charitable purpose: program-related investments (PRIs). Defined in the U.S. tax code, PRIs are investments—including below-market-rate loans, guarantees, linked deposits, or equity investments—made primarily for an exempt or charitable purpose and not for investment return. They are often structured as unsecured debt, and they must be related to foundations' programs or their mission. PRIs are required, by law, to generate below-market risk-adjusted financial returns, and they cannot be used for political purposes. They were initiated by the Ford Foundation and MacArthur Foundation in the 1960s as an alternative way to invest in social change while earning a modest return. Like grants, PRIs count as qualifying distributions toward the 5 percent payout a private foundation is required to make to maintain its tax-exempt status. Because they are based on grants distributed by foundations, once the money is gone, it's truly gone, and the real risk is that the social impact that had been expected from such investment never materializes.

Despite this risk, because the investments on the below-market side of the continuum like PRIs are linked to the missions of foundations and nonprofit organizations, they remain attractive to traditional financial institutions because they meet the requirements placed on banks under the Community Reinvestment Act. They offer a mechanism for banks to show regulators that they are investing in underserved parts of their communities, and meeting these requirements is important to achieving other objectives for which banks wish to earn regulator approval when it comes to growth or entry to new markets.

One other tool is beginning to find its way into the foundation world—the issuance of bonds by foundations to increase their charitable giving. Historically, foundations have not borrowed money but have relied solely on the performance of their endowments. As with the use of foundation endowments to make guarantees, foundations can increase their charitable giving by borrowing against their endowments. The Bush Foundation recently issued $100 million in bonds and used the proceeds to greatly increase grant making in Indian country.

INVESTING BEYOND FINANCIAL RETURN

To fully understand how markets work and why investing for social impact can matter, we must first acknowledge something fundamental about all investments, no matter where they reside on a continuum of risk—the entire nature of world markets is extremely abstract and somewhat arbitrary. When you think about it, as a society we have developed a shared faith that abstract things have value; we produce pieces of paper, whether those are stock certificates, bonds, loan documents, house deeds, or insurance policies, and we reach agreement that they represent monetary value. This is true in part because the entire larger concept of money is also an abstraction, another cultural contract we have entered. A collective of people linked by a shared nationality accept that pieces of paper or coin issued by its governing system have recognizable marketable value.

This is what Alfred North Whitehead labeled the fallacy of misplaced concreteness, recognizing we often mistake an abstract belief, opinion, or concept for a physical or "concrete" reality. Even the gold standard was abandoned in 1914. The human species, with rare exception, has mostly abandoned barter economies and the like; certainly, in American culture, you don't go to your doctor and pay for an appendectomy with the chickens that you raise. We have instead agreed to create regulated financial markets and produced internationally recognized currencies. When I speak at events and conferences on some of the topics raised in this book, I often take a dollar out of my wallet and make a bit of a show by asking the audience what I am holding. Most often the reply is "That's a dollar." "No," I say, "it's a piece of paper," and I rip it in half in front of the audience. More often than not, the audience is stunned. Some people are appalled at seeing me, in their eyes, damage "legal tender." And of course, to be clear, I always keep both halves and tape the bill back together again so that it remains legal tender. Yet audience members react with alarm because we have created a system that's become embedded in our beliefs that the physical bill holds value. (The rise of cryptocurrency is leading to an even deeper level of abstraction. I acknowledge that cryptocurrencies exist, but I will not focus on them any further in this book.) Ultimately, our paper money holds value simply because we agree that it does. At the end of the day, when seen in a certain light, we trade in promises.

It is not insignificant that the root instrument of credit dating back to ancient China is the promissory note—a promise by one party to pay another party a definite sum of money at a specified future date. If we see money for what it is—a cultural contract containing implicit value—then the financial instruments with which we exchange and invest money are tacit agreements about value too. Should we then be surprised that the ways in which we determine if someone is creditworthy are based on opinions, values, perceptions, and assumptions? While we have collectively reached a tacit agreement that what we call money and what we name credit have value, we act quite arbitrarily on how we see "value" in people. Moreover, the word "credit" is derived from the Latin word "credo," which means trust or belief. Humans are guilty of a kind of tribalism—feeling most comfortable among those they already know and trust or who seem a lot like them. The market discounts the character of people it doesn't know. For ages, among the people financial institutions didn't "know" were women, for only as recently as 1974 and the passage of the Equal Credit Opportunity Act, women in this country were not allowed to have credit cards issued in their own name. The same act prohibited credit discrimination on the basis of qualities like race, religion, age, and others. Fifty years is a blip of time in a historical continuum. A lot has changed since 1974, but much has not. If people of color remain severely underrepresented as employees in the financial industry, should we be surprised that there is also unequal representation of racial minorities as customers? Within the banking/credit subsector of finance where people of color have the highest representa-

> IF WE SEE MONEY FOR WHAT IT IS—A CULTURAL CONTRACT CONTAINING IMPLICIT VALUE—THEN THE FINANCIAL INSTRUMENTS WITH WHICH WE EXCHANGE AND INVEST MONEY ARE TACIT AGREEMENTS ABOUT VALUE TOO.

tion among officials and managers, the numbers still illustrate an undeniable gap; the percentage of officials/managers by race is as follows: Black 7, Hispanic 5, Asian 4.3, American Indian 0.3.[48] Factor in similar disproportionate statistics when examining American consumers who have no credit scores at all, and clearly we still have a financial system where those extending credit don't know the full diversity of the communities they are supposed to serve.

Seen in the light of culturally agreed-upon monetary systems, secured investments make far greater sense than even something as ubiquitous as paper cash, for if we hold tangible assets—like houses, cars, and manufacturing equipment—as collateral, we have created a far less abstract exchange: I'm extending you credit in full knowledge that if you don't pay me back on the terms upon which we agreed, these collateralized assets legally transfer to me. This is the collateralized "promise" of most large transactions, and it is enforced by laws and rules that govern our credit system.

There is a tremendous irony when we recognize that the root of most of our transactions, including the cash we carry, is based on abstract value because we are also a culture that explicitly says with regularity that we value things like love and family. But these sorts of concepts are not provided monetary value. Yet, in actuality, we are forever associating love and family with financial health. Ask nearly any parent why they have worked so hard all their lives to save money or build a business or buy a home, and they will tell you they have done so to make their children's lives better. Moreover, a great deal of familial wealth is passed from one generation to the next, and businesses large and small typically have their roots in a family-owned enterprise,

---

48   The U.S. Equal Employment Opportunity Commission, "Special Report: Diversity in the Finance Industry," updated April 25, 2006, https://www.eeoc.gov/special-report/diversity-finance-industry.

one that parents often hope to pass along to their children and at the least wish for their children to benefit from the equity established. It is most certainly true that when younger generations are looking to take action on an entrepreneurial idea, they turn to family, understanding that the power of love can also be utilized for familial financial invest-ment. There's a funny cliché that says most entrepreneurs raise money from founders, family, friends, and fools. For those who don't have the financial ability to own a home and use its equity to borrow against, family, or the occasional fool, may be their only source of capital. Yet in most models of risk management, love, or other abstract concepts like hard work, commitment, and good ideas, don't easily plug into the data on which investment decisions are made. Grit, love, and faith aren't currencies that banks recognize.

Most financial institutions use the five "Cs" when it comes to determining credit risk: character, capital, capacity, collateral, and conditions. While lenders view character as the most important of the five Cs, it is often measured using credit scores or other metrics of credit history rather than other character traits that cannot be easily quantified. Among those who finance social ventures and represent the below-market side of the continuum, we add a sixth C: community impact. As a culture we hold stereotypes that assume someone who earns a low income would never repay borrowed funds. We tend to view being poor as a choice or a character flaw. I suspect we all like to believe we do not cast such judgments, but I wonder how honest we are being with ourselves. Even if we genuinely try not to judge others, we are probably guilty of certain assumptions. Perhaps assumptions are present in the views more experienced people hold toward the younger, less experienced (or vice versa) or in something as simple as how one is expected to dress when attending a formal function. Fair-minded or not, we are probably not immune to the occasional disconnect between how we wish to see others and how we instinctively react. Part of this is simply because there is a measurable distance between sympathy and empathy; sympathy involves understanding from one's own perspective, whereas empathy involves an ability to put oneself in another's shoes.

Empathetic or sympathetic to those who have historically been denied full access to capital markets, certainly most of us are slow to recognize how often the deck is stacked against them. Data-driven assessment devices cannot venture into the character of the borrower. Nor are they effective at examining the conditions of specialty markets or the capacity of low-income communities to support business ventures they need or value. CDFIs are different from other financial institutions not just in the way they structure deals along the continuum, but because they take time to try to understand the people with whom they do business. They invest time, and they use tools that don't fit the model of a traditional vision of expediency.

Organizations like CRF thrive in environments where customers are assessed by more than the data attached to them, just as they are expert at linking networks of socially minded financial institutions and creating innovative investment ventures, thereby accelerating the flow of capital and supporting new economic opportunity. For example, in the PPP program, partnership took the form of CRF organizing a network of CDFIs whose borrowers were too small to get loans from banks. All told, CRF originated more than $700 million in loans, mostly to very small businesses. The median loan size was $21,000—a lifeline to many families whose livelihoods were tied to those businesses. The ability of CDFIs to come together to fill the breach is a testament to their role in the country's financial system.

Such concepts go against the grain of those trained within traditional financial institutions. I remember very early on in the history of CRF I had the opportunity to talk with Harvey Golub, who was the CEO of what is now known as Ameriprise. I started describing what we were doing, thinking he of all people would understand this concept of social investing. Almost immediately he stopped me and asked, "Is this business or is this philanthropy?" I said, "It's a spectrum." "No," he replied, "it's got to be one or the other."

That conversation wasn't at all different from one I had with a high-level banking executive. After explaining the concept of what we were trying to do, I added, "You know, there's a human drive for love and affection that can motivate where people put their money. They do it all the time. They invest in the people they love."

He looked shocked. Looking askance at me, he asked, "Do you really think we can build a market on love and affection?"

Recalling an earlier part of our conversation where he had told me about his family, I said, "You are. You said you were helping your son-in-law."

"That's to set up a dental practice," he said, as if it were an entirely different order of business from anyone else in the world.

"That's love and affection," I reminded him. "The question is how do we institutionalize it in markets?"

At its heart, investing in social enterprises is an extension of this idea, one where rather than being solely focused on profit maximization, we see maximization measured by the social impact the investment can have.

But in order for social ventures to be attractive to traditional investors, we need to use instruments that help mitigate the risk, which is where organizations like CRF and other CDFIs come in. An easy way to think about our role is to consider how it parallels the insurance industry. Insurance companies are willing to insure against nearly every kind of risk, including catastrophic loss, but the higher the risk, the higher the cost. The more the insurer can know about the nature of the risk, the more it can manage it and price it. In the financial world, CRF manages risk by taking the risk of first loss. We are showing potential investors that we have put our own money on the line. CRF pioneered the creation of the first secondary market for small business and affordable housing loans. We were the first to tap the capital markets, issuing asset-backed securities collateralized by community development loans. Our securities have been purchased by mainstream institutional investors (banks, pension funds, and insurance companies) to support projects and businesses serving historically underserved people and communities. By underwriting a loan or helping finance a community program or affordable housing development, we are demonstrating that we've done the kind of homework that makes us comfortable taking the risk, which in turn can attract more risk-averse investors in the knowledge that we will take the first loss.

While the transformed financial market after the Great Recession of 2008 and the more recent economic turmoil during the COVID-19 pandemic have required CRF, alongside other community-focused financial institutions, to take different tactics than securitizations, much of how we manage risk, at least philosophically, is not so different than other risk management strategies. To that end CRF actively participates in three CDFI Fund programs: the Financial Assistance Program, the New Markets Tax Credit Program, and the CDFI Bond Guarantee Program. Together with its wholly owned affiliate, National New Markets Tax Credit Fund, Inc., CRF has received $919.5 million in tax credits, all of which have been deployed as flexible loans for nonprofit and for-profit operating businesses located in low-income communities. In 2013 CRF was named the first qualified issuer (QI) for the CDFI Bond Guarantee Program, and since 2014 we have issued more than $1 billion in bonds on behalf of eight CDFIs. Since 2012 CRF is one of three CDFIs to become a national nondepository SBA 7(a) lender, of which there are only fourteen in the country. We use this guaranteed loan product to fund BIPOC and other underserved entrepreneurs, including women, veterans, and small businesses located in low- and moderate-income areas. We financed more than $1 billion in SBA 7(a) and PPP loans combined.

Our successes have come because CRF, like CDFIs across the country, treats people like human beings rather than data points. Way back in the early days of my career, it's that same spirit that took me to Crookston, Minnesota, a tiny town on the flat plains of an ancient lake bed in the extreme northwest part of the state. I arrived in the middle of a blizzard to meet with its economic development agency committee to help them understand how selling their existing business loans to CRF would help the city to make new loans. They needed liquidity to support redevelopment. They really didn't understand our interest or our model, for the idea that a financial institution could be driven by a desire to see their community thrive again rather than purely to reap profits was an anomaly to them. But the city's economic development director understood what we were trying to do, and sitting in an ice-cold boardroom after inching my way through wind-whipped ground blizzards, he and I were able to enlist the help of some traditional bankers who were members of their board. They explained that they had reached their lending limit because they weren't allowed to overconcentrate their investments and still satisfy their regulators, whereas we were the perfect vehicle to create liquidity for the town so it could rebuild. That frigid boardroom offered the reminder that we need to apply creativity and new investment mechanisms if we are to benefit those who are most in need. The Crookston example is illustrative in many ways, for instruments like city-issued bonds tend to be stable, not because they are well collateralized but because the reputation of the city creates value and because the prediction of future value via the tax base offers a mechanism for repayment.

In the years since then, the industry has matured in nearly every way imaginable, particularly since the creation of CDFIs in 1994 by the Riegle Community Development and Regulatory Improvement Act. Along the way the mechanisms for rating CDFIs and the financial products they have created have matured as well. Aeris, a CDFI rating agency, emerged along the way, and many

> **PERCEIVED RISK IS NOT NECESSARILY ACTUAL RISK..**

of the funds developed by various CDFIs have received Standard and Poor's A+ and even AAA ratings. Standard and Poor's, among others, now has formalized mechanisms for providing ESG evaluations across all industries. In short, investors now have the means through third-party validation to assess risk among those organizations leading social ventures and make informed decisions.

Organizations that are focused on accomplishing social and community impacts can take the risks that banks won't, and sometimes the risk/reward continuum creates investments that can have their part in helping bring positive change to entire communities. Whether developing a securitization or creating a capital stack in a specific partnership or putting government money to work through SBA loans, our industry has learned how to manage risk very effectively. And, along the way, we have learned that perceived risk is not necessarily actual risk. Much of what remains an ongoing need is one of education in the marketplace about what CDFIs are and what they can accomplish, for when people understand the risk they're taking, they'll invest. And increasingly, as we have discussed, investors want to invest in social enterprises.

CHAPTER 6

WHAT CHANGED WITH GEORGE FLOYD'S MURDER

If a great deal of risk assessment within financial markets is about perception, there has long been a perception that historically underinvested communities are high risk. If individuals go looking to confirm such bias against investment in low-income communities, it's not hard to find data that appear to support this perception—higher violent crime rates, more property crimes, higher percentages of people experiencing homelessness, poorer school attendance and graduation rates. For many, data such as these lead them to avoid investment. But at least three vital things are missed in this reaction: 1) how such perception is not only generalized and narrow-minded, but it also helps form a self-fulfilling reality; 2) how many of the roots of such negative externalities reside in sweeping though fixable systemic problems; and 3) how perception often blindfolds the realization that community investment can be transformative. The very characteristics that are associated with communities seen as desirable—strong social organization, youth job opportunities, and residential stability, to name three features—are exactly what business development and affordable housing help create and support.

We encountered reluctance among investors in the Twin Cities when we collaborated with local banks to make more than one hundred subordinate loans to support businesses along Franklin Avenue and Lake Street in south Minneapolis. Like the entrepreneurs who make up the Midtown Global Market, most of the businesses involved were small enterprises run by locals. Again and again as we explained our objectives to potential investors, we encountered people saying, "Crime drives out development," to which we continuously replied, "Development drives out crime." The lending that emerged from the public/private partnerships in which we participated helped spark the revitalization of the Phillips, Seward, and Powderhorn Park neighborhoods just as we had predicted and as similar development around the country has accomplished, in this case resulting in a 62 percent decline in crime rates from 1998 to 2009 and an increase in property values that exceeded the city average. Good investment and mission-driven development create their own entropy, and these kinds of transformations are tangible. As a result not only did civic pride and identity grow in these parts of Minneapolis, but it also spread.

Contrary to conventional, commonplace perception, at CRF we have witnessed firsthand how, provided access to capital and investment, people from underinvested and underestimated communities seize opportunity. With investment, because such communities tend to demonstrate strength of resilience and are sustained by the capable backbones of community-minded organizations, the lives of their citizens undergo notable improvements. Sometimes even microinvestments can change lives for families. The stories of transformation in communities where we have largened opportunity through investment support a long-held view among social entrepreneurs that physical transformation—prominently including affordable housing development—is a powerful platform for change. Neglected buildings and unsightly vacant lots harbor crime and signal disorder. With the presence of renovated homes, new construction on vacant lots, and investment into parks, trails, recreational facilities, and community gardens, newcomers seeking homes choose revitalized neighborhoods as a place to live, and existing residents choose to remain. Better, safer housing and more people with incomes from sustainable local employment construct a foundation for the emergence of more vital business districts, safer streets, and improved schools and public services. A school filled with children from families that feel connected to one another becomes a place of civic pride, one that attracts the best-qualified teachers who are energized by the presence of diversity. Barbershops and salons become informal community gathering places. Restaurants, coffeehouses, and shops begin to feature products sourced locally or that support local artists. Thriving small businesses can begin to support networks of additional businesses, and they can support deep roots within neighborhoods. They can create equity that alters the lives of future generations. An innovative peer CDFI, Local Initiatives Support Corporation, has offered excellent studies comparing data points from neighborhoods in which they have made sizable investments versus similar neighborhoods in the same cities. Their findings support the potency of community transformation that can occur with targeted investment, most noticeably in consistent, and sometimes dramatic, reduction of crime rates. In the nearly thirty years since CDFIs were officially formed by federal legislation, we now have more than a generation of evidence to demonstrate how effective investment in low-income communities can prove—investments that don't just counter conventional wisdom but that earn investors financial returns and the intangible satisfaction in knowing they have played a part in bettering people's lives.

NINE MINUTES, TWENTY-NINE SECONDS

However, history reminds us that progress can be fragile. Even the success we saw through the partnership that brought new vitality to the Phillips, Seward, and Powderhorn Park neighborhoods offers tragic testimony about how quickly good work can be swept away. In those neighborhoods of south Minneapolis, it only took nine minutes and twenty-nine seconds to dramatically alter the short-term outlook for the community.

Nine minutes and twenty-nine seconds, the duration of time that police officer Derek Chauvin kneeled on George Floyd's neck, became shorthand around the world as a reference to oppressive racism that so stubbornly remains omnipresent despite laws guaranteeing equal opportunity and gains in leadership positions by Black and Brown individuals within government and business. George Floyd's murder galvanized mainstream discourse. And in some of the expressions of anguish, many south Minneapolis neighborhoods were set ablaze with civil unrest.

Perhaps it was the nine minutes and twenty-nine seconds. Perhaps it was the video record. Perhaps it was George Floyd's final words: "I can't breathe," words that sounded as a metaphorical experience to so many people of color. Perhaps it was because the number of Black Americans dying of COVID-19 was so radically disproportionate to the rest of the population. Perhaps it was that everything, even murder, has a breaking point. In the aftermath of George Floyd's death, it felt like something had changed and there might be an opportunity for people to come together to finally demand equity for all. It's with this hope that I believe we will come to see the short-term rebuilding needs as a difficult but necessary precursor to the uncomfortable conversations and actions we need to take to root out systemic inequity.

Or perhaps not. Will our collective memory of George Floyd fade? It is worth reminding ourselves that George Floyd's death was one in a chain of other murders of unarmed Black people just in the months immediately before and after May 25, 2020: Manuel Ellis, Breonna Taylor, Ahmaud Arbery, and Andre Hill are among the more publicized cases that sparked a national conversation. Their names were added to a long list of names that will likely feel familiar if distant, a list so long that it gives us pause: Tamir Rice, Michael Brown, Eric Garner; or perhaps you recall the names of Eric Harris, Walter Scott, Freddie Gray, and William Chapman. Maybe some among us know their names. Do we know their lives? Do we understand their communities? Did we know their dreams? I have worked throughout my career as a social entrepreneur focused on helping underinvested communities gain access to financial capital to which they have so long been denied, yet when I hear the echoes of the names I learned on the nightly news in my childhood and youth—Medgar Evers, James Chaney, Malcolm X, Martin Luther King Jr.—I wonder just how far we have progressed.

> **RACISM VIOLATES LIVES, OUR VALUES, AND OUR VISION OF WHAT IS FAIR AND JUST. IT VIOLATES THE FUNDAMENTAL HUMAN RIGHT TO EQUALITY. RACISM DENIGRATES THE EQUAL WORTH OF CITIZENS.**

Racism violates lives, our values, and our vision of what is fair and just. It violates the fundamental human right to equality. Racism denigrates the equal worth of citizens. This is as true when racism is present in the financial industry as it is when acts of violence are the result. In the last chapter, I detailed how the system we have set up in the United States for efficiently making credit decisions relies on data that exclude a large number of people who have not traditionally had the opportunities to develop strong credit profiles. I also delineated the still widening racial wealth gap. Both sets of facts depict a historical, and systemic, system of economic racial inequity.

Consider a slightly broader economic profile than what we have already covered. In 2010 Black Americans made up 13 percent of the population but had only 2.7 percent of the country's wealth. The median net worth for a White family was $134,000, but the median net worth for a Hispanic family was $14,000, and for a Black family it was $11,000. The median wealth for a single White woman has been measured at $41,000, while for Hispanic women it was $140 and for Black women $120.[49] People of color make up about 40 percent of the U.S. population but only own 20 percent of the nation's 5.6 million businesses with employees.[50] Women represent 51 percent of the U.S. population but only 33 percent of business owners with employees, a disparity ratio of 65 percent.[51] To paraphrase the words of Hollywood executive Shonda Rhimes, supporting groups so starkly underrepresented is not diversifying but rather normalizing representation.

As we have recognized elsewhere, much of the dearth of those opportunities has roots in systemic racism. But exactly what is systemic racism? How does it create unconscious bias? Why does it remain so stubbornly present in our culture?

49   Race Forward, Center for Social Inclusion, "What Is Systemic Racism," https://www.raceforward.org/videos/systemic-racism.

50   Economic Growth Engine for Memphis and Shelby County, "Brookings: Businesses Owned by Women and Minorities Have Grown. Will COVID-19 Undo That?" https://www.growth-engine.org/news/brookings-businesses-owned-by-women-and-minorities-have-grown-will-covid-19-undo-that/.

51   Economic Growth Engine, "Brookings."

It can be hard for some to understand what terms like "systemic," "structural," or "institutionalized inequality" even mean. I myself have been on a multidecade journey of learning and understanding. Growing up in my all-White enclave, I was told to lock my car doors and windows in Black neighborhoods. When I ran for a city council seat in 1978, I knocked on the doors of many of the people I'd been told to fear or at the very least ignore. And over the last half century, I've learned from neighbors and colleagues and friends in their own words what systemic discrimination has meant for them and their families. And still, as a White man, I will never experience systemic racism the way so many people in this country are forced to face it because of the color of their skin. I felt something akin to racism when, after my beloved wife's death, I began to allow myself to embrace the fuller sexual feelings I repressed but had experienced for as long as I can remember. In a business environment where many of those I worked among held strong to what they might label as "traditional values" that included prescriptive views on LGBTQ individuals, I was quite aware of the judgment passed by some when I began appearing at functions in the company of the man who now has been my partner for the past nine years. Of course, my experiences are different from those of my Black, Brown, and Indigenous friends because they cannot hide the color of their skin.

Still there is pain in what I long believed I needed to hide. For LGBTQ people there exists a societal pressure to not be who you are. It is hard to describe the toll enacted upon someone when they have to maintain a secret that they don't fully understand, something I felt from adolescence. I lived in fear that if my secret were revealed, others would not love me. I was lucky that I had decades with a woman I loved with all my heart and that we raised two remarkable daughters, yet those secrets and fears remained part of me. The simple reality was that had I acted on my feelings, for much of my life I would have been in violation of the law. Today, Oliver and I are, at least in our home state of Minnesota, protected by laws that disallow discrimination against LGBTQ people in employment, housing, and public accommodations. That certainly is not the case everywhere. Nor do state or federal laws necessarily stop actions of systemic bias. I do not equate my experience to that of BIPOC people, nor even to the experience of my partner, who is Vietnamese and came to the U.S. as a refugee and is now a nephrologist, but it does help me understand some aspects of others who face the organized suppression of their rights.

For my Black friends, colleagues, and clients, such suppression was, of course, formalized via slavery and Jim Crow laws, in racist policies like redlining, and in the poorly masked racism that erected barriers for Black Americans in science, medicine, and education. Barriers were also constructed for nearly all non-White immigrant populations at varying points of U.S. history. The laws or policies may have changed, but those changes didn't automatically dismantle all the barriers that went along with them.

In a simple but remarkably instructive TikTok video titled "The Fence" by stand-up comedian Ta'Vi, the nature of how systemic racism works is cleverly revealed. She imagines two people on opposite sides of a fence that has been there longer than either can remember. All the fruit trees grow on one side of the fence. When people on the barren side of the fence complain they are hungry and ask those on the other side to throw them some fruit, they are met with a number of responses including things like, "A person once successfully climbed the fence; why don't you?" The response is, "I tried, but I'm so weak from not eating that I didn't make it," which generates the reply, "Why don't you just try again?"

The people who have an abundance of fruit complain that they have to pick the fruit in order to eat it and question why they should just give it away, and then they suggest that all they hear from the other side are complaints about the fence when they aren't the ones who built it. When the hungry people suggest that they just take the fence down, they are met with the objection, "Our ancestors built this fence." That generates a response from the hungry people that "you must really love this fence." Those who are blissfully full of fruit take offense and shout, "Don't you dare call us fence lovers," which initiates a raucous argument that descends into insults. Once things calm down, those on the fruit tree side of the fence suggest that maybe they could send some seeds over, but after they are met with the response that "fruit trees take a long time to grow, and we are starving now," they return to the tactic of insults and accuse those on the other side of being "lazy and impatient."[52]

Sound familiar? We might all recognize that telling people to plant their own trees or tear down the fence themselves would be rightfully interpreted as a cruel response rather than helpful if one considers the lived reality on the other side. The idea of what is fair requires that we take that lived reality (remembering that even among the compassionate, empathy can be difficult when your own reality is quite different) and history into account. In Ta'Vi's metaphor, the hungry people's ancestors were probably the ones who planted the fruit trees in the first place, something that allows the metaphor to apply through a historical racial lens (so much of the foundation of this country's wealth was built on the backs of unpaid, enslaved Black people) or a wealth inequality lens (underpaid working-class laborers

---

52   Ta'Vi, "The Fence," tavitalkstrash, TikTok, June 9, 2021, https://www.tiktok.com/foryou?is_from_webapp=v1&item_id=6971940986821872902#/@tavitalkstrash/video/6971940986821872902.

as being exploited by obscenely wealthy business owners in the name of capitalism).

One vestige of this history is the commonplace and stubborn reality of profiling. Sometimes blatant, sometimes a matter of unconscious bias, our culture continues to make determinations—and, too often, policies—on the basis of systemically driven perceptions. As I learned firsthand from conversations that emerged among my colleagues in the immediate aftermath on the day of George Floyd's murder, "driving while Black" is a ubiquitous experience for most of my Black coworkers, friends, and family members. A few years ago, as I was driving from Brooklyn to Manhattan late after dropping my daughters at their homes in Williamsburg, I stopped at a red light in Greenpoint where there was no other traffic. When the light turned green, I advanced through the intersection, and suddenly a police car that had been parked with its lights off turned on its siren and pulled me over. As I sat in my car waiting, two officers approached the car— one on either side—and scared the daylights out of me! I asked the officers, "What did I do wrong?" They responded that I had not stopped "behind the line" at the intersection. This traffic stop was clearly a pretextual stop in order to carry out New York City's infamous "stop and frisk policy." When the officers saw I was White and dressed in a business suit, they let me go. Had I been a Black man, I am certain the police would have frisked me. I have never experienced the fear such a moment ignites in my Black friends or had reason to think, "What are they going to accuse me of doing wrong?" or "Will they draw a weapon on me?" These types of pretextual traffic stops for minor infractions such as air fresheners

> **THERE HAS BEEN A "PRETEXTUAL STOP" MADE IN DECIDING PEOPLE'S FINANCIAL FATES.**

on a rearview mirror or improperly signaling a turn have long been sources of tension in the Black community, and too often they have led to deaths, as was the case with Philando Castile and, more recently, Daunte Wright.

Connecting to the financial world, too often sources of tension have found their equivalent in the faces of White male bankers sitting on the opposite side of a desk, where there has been a "pretextual stop" made in deciding people's financial fates. I am entirely aware that as a White man not only have I led a privileged life, but I have also had opportunities that have placed me in positions to help make change happen. It is precisely others like me who have the power of credit-making decisions who must lead change to extinguish systemic racist practices inside the financial industry, explicit or otherwise.

A national history of overt racism built into our institutions has created a legacy of unjust racial treatment that has outlived legal attempts to remove discrimination and lingers within institutions and systems. This history has created a climate of understandable distrust. Tiffany Howard, writing for the Center for Policy Analysis and Research in a report written for the Congressional Black Caucus Foundation, sums up this history and its impact with more eloquence than I can:

> The legacy of slavery, Jim Crow laws, and repeated civil rights violations, have eroded the trust of African Americans in the government, U.S. institutions, and social interactions for over a century. And this lack of trust is also reinforced by the negative experiences African Americans have with financial institutions when unsuccessfully attempting to secure a business startup loan. Improving trust within the Black community and cracking down on institutional discrimination is essential to building Black social capital and producing

more successful African American entrepreneurs. There are no simple or quick solutions to address the level of social distrust among African Americans because it has been cultivated over four centuries of contact with U.S. institutions.[53]

Whether intentional in their bias or not, many financial institutions have deeply entrenched policies and behaviors that create inequitable treatment. Over time the effects of data-driven decisions and biased behavior have had dire, multigenerational consequences. They have driven families out into the streets to face instability and uncertainty. They have quashed dreams and quelled educations. Just as anywhere, and I hope rare, within such institutions there remain individuals who are also open and inhumane in acting on personal racist beliefs. More often people within institutions are not racist but do sustain racist policies or imbalanced treatment of certain classes identified by gender, sexuality, immigration status, or disability—perhaps ignorantly unaware they are doing so. Institutions that fail to address systemic racism actively are more likely to unconsciously foster its legacy. Individuals who might accurately describe themselves as supportive of diversity and inclusion may be unaware of more nuanced cultural histories or ignorant about inherently discriminatory processes and policies. Systemically racist policies and procedures result in debasing experiences, frustration, and heartache for those who are treated as "different." It would be inappropriate to equate the torturous death of George Floyd to declined bank loans, but at the cultural center of both policing and banking is a complex web of long-standing systemic injustices that too often impede the life, liberty, and pursuit of happiness for Americans of color.

---

53   Tiffany Howard, "The State of Black Entrepreneurship in America: Evaluating the Relationship between Immigration and Minority Business Ownership," Center for Policy Analysis and Research, April 10, 2019, https://www.cbcfinc.org/wp-content/uploads/2019/05/CPAR-Report-Black-Entrepreneurship-in-America.pdf, 19.

A MODEL OF SYSTEMIC RACISM—AND A SOLUTION

The consequences of systemic discrimination would have been unavoidably visible when driving nearly any street of residential Detroit in the years following 2008 when thousands of houses sat empty or neglected or disappeared altogether with the push of a bulldozer. The Great Recession hit the entire nation hard but walloped Detroit, which has one of the highest percentages of Black people in the country. What happened in Detroit in the wake of the recession offers a useful sort of informal case study about the linkages between race, financial hardship, and the pure-profit mentality that dominates markets. Images of 14688 Hazelridge Street, as noted by Alex Alsup of Loveland Technologies, show the consequences in stark relief.[54] In just five years, this section fell into decay, homes were torn down, and foliage began to grow over the sidewalks.

What were the forces that created this disintegration of Detroit neighborhoods? America's eleventh-largest city has been bleeding people for years. Its population, which peaked at 1.85 million in 1950, was halved to 917,000 by 2008, fueled by enormous layoffs in the automotive industry. That flight has continued, and the 2020 census showed that the city's population had further reduced to 637,601.[55] In this iconic city associated with the power of American technology and industry through much of the twentieth century, today more than a third of its residents live below the poverty line.[56] In the late 1990s and early 2000s, the city was at the forefront of ill-fated U.S. efforts

---

54   Julia La Roche, "Google Street View Images Show the Incredible Amount of Decay in Detroit Just since 2008," *Business Insider*, May, 30, 2014, https://www.businessinsider.com/detroit-home-photos-2014-5.

55   PopulationU, "Detroit Population," https://www.google.com/search?q=Detroit+populaiton+Population+U.com&rlz=1C1VIQF_enUS970US971&oq=Detroit+populaiton+Population+U.com&aqs=chrome..69i57j33i10i160l3j33i299l2.9450j1j7&sourceid=chrome&ie=UTF-8.

56   Welfare Info, "Poverty in Detroit, Michigan," https://www.welfareinfo.org/poverty-rate/michigan/detroit.

to encourage homeownership among lower-income residents. Some home buyers were lulled into unsuitable deals by predatory lenders. Regulation was appallingly lax. According to the *Detroit News*, just twelve examiners were responsible for overseeing Michigan's 2,800 mortgage companies in 2008.[57] While it is true that some borrowers behaved recklessly by taking on mortgages they could not afford, intending to refinance a year or two down the road, many others were enticed by the appeal of purchasing homes for the first time in their lives or bettering their lot with improved housing. As the housing crisis hit, many were left unable to meet their mortgage obligations. Foreclosures ran rampant.

Laden with thousands of vacant Detroit homes, banks became desperate to sell, accepting a pittance simply to avoid ballooning bills for maintenance and security of empty homes on which they had foreclosed. These homes were the poster children for the nationwide write-offs that plagued Wall Street and crippled institutions such as Lehman Brothers and Bear Stearns. Home values plunged so low—half the city's sales were under $10,000—that the city largely became a cash-based market. Appraisers could not create accurate comparisons despite there existing sizable numbers of potential home buyers with good credit and stable employment history. This lack of ability to secure financing forced many families either to pay cash, something that was impossible for most, or to pay rent rather than have the opportunity to build equity and invest in their futures. Instead, they had to live at the demands of landlords that had entered the market cheaply but now controlled pricing of a needed commodity. The true "growth industry" in Detroit in the years following 2008 was demo-

---

57   Christine MacDonald and Joel Kurth, "Foreclosures Fuel Detroit Blight, Cost City $500 Million," *Detroit News*, June, 3, 2015, https://www.detroitnews.com/story/news/special-reports/2015/06/03/detroit-foreclosures-risky-mortgages-cost-taxpayers/27236605/.

lition. The houses banks were willing to sell rather than demolish, often for four figures, went mostly to investors who seldom completed repairs and exploited Detroit's lower-income residents by charging high rents. Huge corporations and smaller real estate entrepreneurs alike, all with cash holdings, became landlords—usually invisible or absentee landlords—to people who had once owned their own homes. As Alsup's images demonstrate, banks typically decided to sell to those who saw huge profitability in the rental market or simply left properties to slowly deteriorate. Crime, including theft of the few commodities of value from such properties, like copper plumbing, swept through once-vibrant neighborhoods. Squatters took up residence in partially destroyed, abandoned homes.

The predatory lending practices that started this housing crisis impacted Black people and other racial minorities at far higher rates than Whites. Analyzing the data that support such a statement, something I will do more of in a moment, offers evidence that such practices are not isolated and that they point to policies and approaches that exist throughout the system.

Addressing systemic inequality present in housing, in 2021 Avis Jones-DeWeever, executive director of the National Council of Negro Women, analyzed federal data in the Home Mortgage Disclosure Act, which revealed that African Americans and Hispanics were 30 percent more likely to receive high-rate subprime loans compared with White borrowers.[58] Discussing the findings, Jones-DeWeever said, "We are looking at intentional draining of Black wealth that has set us back generations. Driven by the housing crisis, Black wealth has dropped

---

58   Barbara Reynolds, "Minorities Fall Victim to Predatory Lenders," *Washington Post* Blogs, July 16, 2012, https://www.washingtonpost.com/blogs/therootdc/post/minorities-fall-victim-to-preda-tory-lenders/2012/07/16/gJQAraMYpW_blog.html.

fifty-two percent in four years during the recession, which is the largest loss of Black wealth since Reconstruction following the Civil War."[59]

In Detroit the predatory practices that targeted racial minorities were further exacerbated by a lax regulatory system that resulted in wholly inaccurate appraisals. This should come as no surprise. The bias present against Black and Hispanic homeowners and prospective homeowners is often captured in differential appraisal values and other systemic measures. A 2021 analysis by Freddie Mac found that the appraisal value of homes in predominantly Black and Hispanic neighborhoods is oftentimes much lower than that of houses in mostly White communities. Researchers found that 12.5 percent of homes appraised in Black communities were valued at less than the original cost of constructing the home. That figure compares to 7.4 percent of homes in White neighborhoods and 9.4 percent of homes in Latino areas.[60] Such differences, much like zoning restrictions that make single-family homes dominant in suburbs, extend a kind of de facto redlining.

Zoning restrictions and similar phenomena are prime examples of how racism can become systemic. A key and common example is what occurs when we tie school funding to local property taxes. Communities that raise more money in property taxes have more money for schools. Necessarily, lower-income neighborhoods have schools that must make do with substantially different budgets than districts in wealthier sections of the same city. This long-accepted school-funding mechanism enforces racial segregation. Doing so creates other scenarios in which those who may not see themselves as racists take actions that categorize people and treat them unequally. A prime

---

59   Reynolds, "Minorities Fall Victim."

60   Khristopher J. Brooks, "There's a Big 'Appraisal Gap' between Black and White Homeown-ers," Moneywatch, CBS News, September 24, 2021, https://www.cbsnews.com/news/freddie-mac-home-appraisal-housing-discrimination-black-homeowner/.

example is how real estate agents sometimes steer potential buyers into specific parts of the city, often without consciously knowing they are doing so. There might be neighborhoods where they won't even show homes to people of color by acting on their own implicit bias. A White broker might even believe that they are doing their client a favor by showing them homes in neighborhoods where there are majorities of residents of the same racial background, or they may simply believe that some neighborhoods will prove more hostile to a potential buyer; either action represents what we might label a kind of "spatial racism," one that is frequently passed on from one agent to another and from one generation to the next.

CREATING SYSTEMS SOLUTIONS FOR SYSTEMIC PROBLEMS

So how do we solve the inequities that result from systemic racism?

I invite you to think about the metaphor of a fence dividing those who have and those who have not. While the idea of sharing seeds from an abundance of fruit in order for others to produce their own orchards is neither inherently wrong nor severely distanced from the ways in which I have advocated for creating velocity in capital markets, it still denies that substantial and complex barriers exist in the first place, and it fails to account for the time required to build meaningful wealth or to overcome the exponential generational effects of disadvantages. Social enterprises have made positive differences in individual lives with regularity and have nudged change forward for whole communities, but their scale simply has never reached what is necessary to dismantle persistent existing barriers or ensure that, to return to Ta'Vi's metaphor, the soil is sufficiently fertilized and that there is enough food to maintain people through the time it takes for an orchard to reach productivity.

To dismantle systemic racism within institutions, equity-based policies must not only investigate, adjudicate, and learn from individual cases of wrongdoing, but they must also proactively prevent them through vigilant systems of recruitment, the reformation of policies, programs and training, substantive diversity and leadership initiatives, antibias training and education, community liaison, and regular institutional review.

I remain confident we can help make change happen. But it is an uphill battle, for systemic racism remains entrenched in all aspects of our society. As the George Floyd case reminded us, we're sadly familiar with the realities of institutional racism in law enforcement. In the financial industry, there are multiple regulations that were written with the aim of rooting out discrimination, yet bias remains embedded in fissures throughout the system. Like people everywhere, loan officers and mortgage brokers apply systems that are based on inaccurate assumptions. When financial institutions make decisions based upon failed algorithms meant as one-size-fits-all expediencies, they act in the same patterns that created redlining in the first place. Worse still, we have witnessed how some in finance justified providing customers access to easy credit at unsustainable interest rates, whether in shameless pursuit of pure profit or to justify their actions in the belief they had helped working-class people of little means expand homeownership. Whatever the explanation of motive, such actions created the subprime mortgage crisis nationwide that so devastated Detroit. Yet an example like Detroit's housing crisis can teach us how we can use an entrepreneurial spirit of innovation to help solve financial inequities. Out of this disaster, creative minds within the

CDFI world envisioned what became the Detroit Home Mortgage (DHM) program.

If Detroit offered a case study on the effects of predatory lending, it also offers a living example of the kinds of change that can come from the creative spirit of cooperative ventures often stewarded by CDFIs. At the urging of Detroit mayor Mike Duggan, a diverse group of partners including the Obama administration's Detroit Federal Working Group, Clinton Global Initiative, and local banks, foundations, and nonprofits including the Kresge Foundation, the Ford Foundation, and the Michigan State Housing Development Authority joined forces to find a solution to the appraisal and financing gap. Led by CRF, a group of partners developed this innovative program aimed to increase homeownership and reinvestment in Detroit's neighborhoods. Detroit Home Mortgage addressed the appraisal value gap associated with the renovation of properties by combining a second mortgage with a conventional first mortgage to assist in funding rehabilitated single-family properties. The end goal was to increase the number of mortgages, eventually bringing back the conventional mortgage market and making Detroit Home Mortgage unnecessary.

> *IF DETROIT OFFERED A CASE STUDY ON THE EFFECTS OF PREDATORY LENDING, IT ALSO OFFERS A LIVING EXAMPLE OF THE KINDS OF CHANGE THAT CAN COME FROM THE CREATIVE SPIRIT OF COOPERATIVE VENTURES.*

DHM was launched in 2016. Through this collaborative effort to address financial gaps in appraisals, borrowers could afford to buy, renovate, and occupy homes that otherwise would go to cash investors or bank repossession. DHM was designed as a temporary market intervention to increase the number of mortgages throughout the city by laying the groundwork for real, negotiated appraisals in real estate transactions. In this regard the program is a reminder about the nature of risk, for the risk here was found in mispricing collateral. DHM served as a catalyst to determine the true value of the home. As a result neighborhoods throughout the city saw increases in the availability of mortgages. Demonstrating the true spirit of mission-driven social enterprises aiming for long-term customer success, DHM required borrowers to take two different training courses to obtain their mortgage product. The first was a high combined loan-to-value course that explained market conditions along with the pros and cons of the program. For the second requirement, people could choose between a Department of Housing and Urban Development or a Michigan State Housing Development Authority–approved home buyer education course. For properties requiring renovation, a renovation course taught DHM borrowers about the roles necessary for success. And what a success. In the three years from 2016 to 2019, approved mortgage rates doubled. Set to end in 2019, DHM was such a success that all the partners involved signed on to extend the program for two more years. The program stopped making new mortgages early in 2022.

What can we learn from programs like DHM? How can we make meaningful change happen for those who possess the desire and the drive to become homeowners and business owners but who have been left out of American prosperity? Can the momentum from the sweeping, pluralistic call for change as aroused by George Floyd's murder and other related events from the spring and summer of 2020 help propel a sustained movement, one that attracts investors and other active participants not already supporting marginalized communities in impactful ways? Can capitalism hold answers for change rather than continuing to erect barriers for racial minorities?

ARE WE LIVING IN A MOMENT THAT CAN SUMMON CHANGE?

We have to return to the question I posed earlier: Has George Floyd's murder changed anything? I remain hopeful that out of yet another tragedy, change will arise. In the end, as someone who is racially and economically privileged, it is not my place to make a full assessment on this front. Further, having committed my life to fomenting positive change within the generally accepted framework of modest reformations to capitalism, I am biased. I have seen the success of CRF's endeavors and the impact it can have on people's lives. But I have also experienced how slow such change has been, how incremental progress tends to be, how remote daily tragedy suffered by others can feel to many, and how quickly we seem to forget the tragedies that infiltrate public consciousness. Beth Marcus, executive vice president of the Local Initiatives Support Corporation, the nation's largest CDFI, estimates it would cost more than $10 trillion to close the racial wealth gap between Black and White U.S. households.[61]

Marcus said that Local Initiatives Support Corporation set a new fundraising record in 2020, enabling it to invest $2 billion into historically underserved communities, paralleling a pattern experienced by other CDFIs, including CRF, and repeated through the kinds of historic commitments to social justice investment made by numerous corporations as I detailed earlier in the book. While the need for investment is vast, as Marcus indicates, it largely remains to be seen how strong the impact of such corporate commitments can be, nor is it easy to know how sincere they have been in their follow-through. Part of the difficulty in assessing corporate follow-through is that most

---

61   Chauncy Alcorn, "George Floyd's Death Was a Wake-up Call for Corporate America. Here's What Has—and Hasn't—Changed," CNN Business, October 7, 2021, https://www.cnn.com/2021/05/25/business/corporate-america-anti-racism-spending/index.html.

initiatives were for multiple years and through complex partnerships with nonprofits.

I have suggested that George Floyd's murder was not different in most ways than any one of thousands of others across time. For me his murder was personal by geographic proximity, much the way the 1967 civil unrest struck me as a youth. It offered a tragic and vivid reminder of how precarious life is for many Americans. I lived in south Minneapolis for many years in neighborhoods close to where George Floyd lost his life. My daily commute in those years placed me on a bus that went right down Chicago Avenue where the George Floyd memorial now stands. I was viscerally repulsed at seeing the video of his murder, horrified that any human could place so little value on another human's life. It wasn't another tragedy in another city elsewhere in my country; it was in my city, in a neighborhood I frequented, one where I had done business and formed relationships. The event of his death and protests that followed, even the withdrawal by an uncertain, challenged police force from historically Black and Brown Minneapolis neighborhoods, underscore the erosion of every-thing that CRF has been trying to do for the last thirty years. The conflagration that occurred in the neighborhoods surrounding the site of George Floyd's murder released untold emotions of anger, fear, and grief across not only south Minneapolis but also the world. But in the days after the murder, an amazing thing happened. Artists, sculptors, and neighbors reclaimed the corner at Thirty-Eighth and Chicago with murals and symbols that began a healing process. I have been touched whenever I visit George Floyd Square, as the art there relates to me personally, not only because of the tragedy, but also because my younger daughter, Lauren, is an artist whose work and practice revolve around using art to cope with grief and to help in the healing process, which has allowed me to witness the hope and catharsis that can come from art centered on remembrance, compassion, and justice.

The people who gather to remember George Floyd are my fellow citizens, and they also come from around the world. Because I live here, I recognize why those who continue to gather daily guard the space in full recognition that it is a sacred place, one that is both real and symbolic simultaneously.

His murder may have come at one of the seismic movements in history when our social fabric reveals its tears but also reveals how it can be mended. Minneapolis has been thrust into a worldwide spotlight, and as a child of the place, one who views it as a progressive community that has often challenged the status quo of the nation, I want to hope my city can prove that it is capable of creating lasting solutions to inequities that have plagued our nation since before it achieved sovereignty. We have witnessed a grassroots response to George Floyd's murder and how his life fits with the larger story of injustice. I believe we can use the tools of inclusive capitalism to make that response achieve lasting change. I take heart in the billions of dollars committed by scores of corporations, including those with origins in Minneapolis, to social justice reform and minority investment. They are like green shoots emerging after a forest fire, a promise of the potential in the future. But we will need time to see if all make good on these commitments and if they sustain them, for it will take sustained investment, continuous commitment to bringing people of color into senior management and board positions, and focused interrogation of corporate policies and procedures. The scale of change needed is massive. CDFIs have demonstrated models that are effective, but honestly, the scale of even our combined efforts has been humble. Band-Aids do not repair arterial bleeding.

I have lived through the Civil Rights Movement. I witnessed the assassinations of Black leaders and those of White leaders who supported them. I applauded the passage of laws guaranteeing justice for all. I saw President Obama elected. Yet every day, as I hear the stories and experiences of my colleagues, of my clients, of the community leaders and nonprofit activists, I am made to realize how far we still have to go. Can this moment be different? Can another injustice change the course of history, or will it be erased by history?

We live in a new age, one where not only is a moment like George Floyd's murder captured in a video but one where that video can be disseminated to the entire world in milliseconds, one where it can be shared and viewed and discussed not only by those in the criminal justice system but also by everyone. We live in a nation where those who are currently in the minority can—slowly and imperfectly to be sure, but visibly—see ever greater representation in the seats of power and commerce where their voices can be amplified. We live in a nation where those who are currently in the minority can identify a foreseeable date on a calendar when they will be in the majority and in a moment when their vote is so important that they must be courted by those who wish to govern. We live in a time when there is ever-increasing pressure from young people everywhere and from other parts of the globe where respect and dignity toward all are seen as an essential right and responsibility. We live in a time when the federal government has budgeted billions of dollars to address systemic racism and to build new infrastructure that can benefit those who have most often been left behind. We live in a time when candidates who advocate for putting capital in the hands of people who historically haven't had it are taken seriously and are provided a national platform to discuss innovative ideas about relationships between financial and social policies. And importantly, in part because all these things are true, we live in a time when asset owners and those who control the flow of capital, not just in the finance industry but in corporations in every sector, are beginning to say that it is time for change.

The specific nature of the democracy we practice in the U.S. goes hand in glove with its application of capitalism. Equity provides the balance that keeps society together. As we undergo a continued erosion of the wealth developed by the middle class over the twentieth century, we risk creating vast economic and social status differences between rich and poor. As a result, shifting support by CEOs and corporate boards for greater diversification in their own make-up and for tangible support of social justice movement, one of the trends I analyzed earlier in this book, is critical to accomplishing change and is as vital as shifts in cultural expectations and the reach of current technologies to speed dissemination of ideas and evolving perceptions. Change is always incremental and evolving, but upheavals, as I have noted, do have identifiable tipping points. George Floyd will not be the last Black man to die at the hands of a police officer. But may it be retrospectively recognized as a critical inflection point that helped remove and reform obstacles to full participation in the American dream for everyone.

CHAPTER 7

MARKETS IN A POST-COVID WORLD

We cannot disentangle George Floyd's murder from another obviously historic, seismic event, the presence of a global pandemic. COVID-19 upended everyone's lives. It has most immediately killed and sickened millions of people. Indirectly, though, it has changed commerce, altered supply chains, overturned the workforce, even challenged some basic assumptions of capitalism and the nature of markets. Employees and employers alike are reimagining the nature of work, its physical location, and its relationship to productivity and personal satisfaction. We have become vividly aware of how intertwined the global marketplace truly is and how fickle and unstable it can quickly become. These realizations occurred congruently with the social upheaval of 2020. One might logically argue that the widescale doubt, confusion, fear, and uncertainty brought into everyone's lives with COVID-19 amplified the emotion of the world witnessing a man protest his innocence and vocalize his pleas of bewilderment as a police officer slowly killed him.

I ended the previous chapter asking questions about sustainable change that might emerge from this social unrest. We must enter this chapter with another set of questions about the future, this time about the changing nature of financial markets. What will the future of finance look like? The future of capitalism? The future of work? I don't pretend to be a prophet, but there are clear trends that have emerged from the fallout of the pandemic.

Here's one thing we have known for some time, even if we have been slow to act upon this knowledge: there is little future in the U.S. economy for repetitive jobs of any sort. Repetitive work is being automated across every industry, including finance. We are moving rapidly beyond the traditional service sector and consumer consumption as the driving forces behind U.S. capitalism. Technological innovation and new industries require new design principles, an agile, well-educated, entrepreneurial-minded workforce, and loads upon loads of data to drive and implement new ideas and new products. We exist within a mature internet ecosystem, are in the midst of the sweeping alterations brought on by both mobile technologies and social media saturation, and are in the fledgling stages of applications for potentially seismic technologies with blockchain and AI.

As Richard Florida argued in his book *The Rise of the Creative Class*, ideas are the currency of the new economy. Florida says that "access to talented and creative people is to modern business what access to coal and iron ore was to steel-making."[62] The reasons for the market shifts I explore in this chapter are complex, cross many disciplines, and have been brought on by commercial, historical, and social changes. For decades manufacturers chased a lower-cost labor force in order to reduce the price of production, expand markets, and deepen

---

62   Richard Florida, *The Rise of the Creative Class* (New York: Basic Books, 2014).

profits. Within and beyond manufacturing, there emerged a growing societal ennui where the conspicuous consumption so common prior to the Great Recession, consumption that was fueled by a need to fill a vast emotional and psychological void left by the absence of meaningful work, no longer held distraction or value.

We spent half a century building international markets and global supply chains mostly to minimize the cost of what remains the largest expense for most businesses—labor. Pursuing returns on investment where profit was king, we stripped away well-paying jobs that once allowed people without college educations to have opportunities to build wealth and enter the middle class. Growing up, my family had a tenuous grasp of a middle-class life due to factors and opportunities much rarer for people with similar education and intergenerational wealth today. In 1968 when my father suffered a stroke, my family nearly lost our home. Because of the physical disabilities resulting from his stroke, my father was never able to work again, and our family finances grew even more tenuous. My parents knew tough times, even putting up their car as collateral for a credit union loan in order to attend our wedding. Those memories remain fresh in my mind and are highly present when I watch the national patterns of financial loss experienced by so many during my lifetime.

In our current century, middle-income Americans have fallen steadily behind where they once stood. "In 2014, the median income of these households was 4% less than in 2000. Moreover, because of the housing market crisis and the Great Recession of 2007–09, median wealth (assets minus debts) fell by 28% from 2001 to 2013."[63]

---

63   Pew Research Center, "The American Middle Class Is Losing Ground," December 9, 2015, https://www.pewresearch.org/social-trends/2015/12/09/the-american-middle-class-is-losing-ground/, paragraph 4.

A byproduct of wage stagnation, millennials face a dire financial situation in comparison to the generations that preceded them.

INTERGENERATIONAL WEALTH [64]

Share of national wealth owned by each generation,
by median cohort age

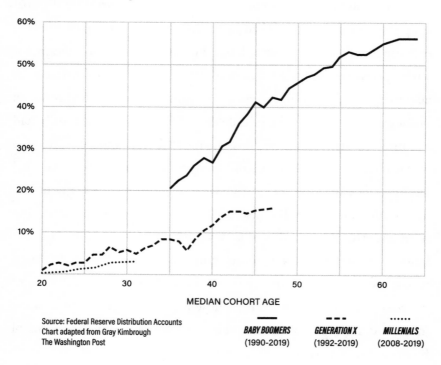

MEDIAN COHORT AGE

Source: Federal Reserve Distribution Accounts
Chart adapted from Gray Kimbrough
The Washington Post

BABY BOOMERS
(1990-2019)

GENERATION X
(1992-2019)

MILLENIALS
(2008-2019)

Warnings of middle-class erosion, wealth stagnation, and the consolidation of extreme wealth by an ever-smaller portion of the total population have come to pass. At the same time when more and more American workers lost jobs to foreign competition and entire industries moved offshore, technological advancements made

---

64   Patrick Donachie, "Illustrating the Wealth Gap between Boomers and Millenni-
      als," WealthManagement.com, December 4, 2019, adapted from a chart developed
      by Gray Kimbrough, https://www.wealthmanagement.com/client-relations/
      illustrating-wealth-gap-between-boomers-and-millennials.

sectors like manufacturing increasingly efficient with ever-smaller workforces. Greater dependency on robotic and artificial intelligence technologies sped production while shedding labor. Repetitive work, whether working an assembly line in a vehicle manufacturing plant, producing piecework in a textile plant, providing clerical support in a business office, or participating in the industrialized process of butchering animals for food supply, among so many others, is quickly becoming a need of the past. Continued development of automation technology—from robotic surgeons to "smart tractors" for planting crops—increasingly reduces or removes labor needs from more and more industries.

This is not a trend. It is a reality, one that will grow. In my hometown, a start-up, Carbon Origins, has developed and is rapidly expanding a market for "Skippy"—a robot controlled by a team of remote operators who use virtual-reality headsets—that picks up and delivers groceries and takeout food. Elsewhere in Minneapolis, Dee Dee is a robot that delivers food and buses tables at Sawatdee, a Thai restaurant. Dee Dee joins a similar robotic worker serving customers at Minneapolis–Saint Paul International Airport. These robots join "TUGs," robots used by a growing number of hospitals that make the rounds of patient food delivery in reducing dependence on low-wage and entry-level workers. Airports and other high-touch, repetitive venues now offer armies of kiosks to augment the work of a handful of staff, a phenomenon akin to the omnipresence of self-checkout at grocery stores and major retailers. Several years ago I saw a demonstration of a robotic cop at the Milken Global Conference. This device was bullet proof, gas proof, and unemotional and had 360-degree cameras. The potential uses and abuses of such technology in light of the previous chapter shouldn't be lost on any of us.

What may appear novelties today will be mainstream in the near future. Do you honestly think that Starbucks won't be replacing baristas if they will increase speed of delivery and lower costs? Will growing consumer demand fueled by COVID-19 policies make grocery and general merchandise retailers stop curbside pickup, or will they replace their current human labor with mechanical interventions? Such devices may be smaller versions than those that fill orders at massive Amazon warehouses, but they are real, and their use is growing rapidly.

And while it is true that blue-collar manufacturing workers became the face of Donald Trump's electorate, the next wave of workers to have technology replace their jobs will increasingly be low-income wage earners, particularly those in service industries, and overwhelmingly that means more and more Black and Brown people and recent immigrants.

They will not be alone. The prevalence of the gig economy—short-term contracts or freelance work rather than permanent jobs—is not a passing phenomenon. Dissatisfaction with work conditions and expectations of more freedom and control over work output have coupled with the presence of new technologies, mobile applications, the availability of remote work, and corporate outsourcing to cut costs in a manner where both the contract worker and the business entity find value. Gig work is tremulous at best, typically for both parties, and will no doubt be refined and restructured. Yet, the nature of the gig economy, certainly for freelance professionals and entrepreneurs taking full advantage of technological invention but often for contract service labor like ride-app drivers and others, supports the agility, curiosity, self-motivation, experimentalism, and fearlessness that are so common to the creative class.

In the recent past, when work was boring, alienating, and dehumanizing, people looked to buy happiness off the shelf. Now they look to create a new future where they can control the work they do and in which they find fulfillment. During the pandemic, educated and technological workers flocked to remote work and virtual meetings, and the appeal of such conditions has rapidly spilled into other sectors. Out-of-work food services employees, for example, have moved into new industries in droves. Emotionally driven consumption is unsustainable, for those trying to fill unfillable voids, for the demands of the marketplace, and for all those left out of choice and opportunity. Too many people have been left behind entirely through a combination of social forces that erect barriers and shifting economics. The educated, the privileged, those who have been provided opportunity to better their lives now flock into this new creative class while those who have earned livings, often paltry livings, with their bodies and technical skills must either seek to retool their abilities or be excised from the workforce altogether.

The modern workforce, like the creative class that is increasingly fueling it, requires far more education. The education might be formal degrees or course-based certificates, but knowledge attainment will be critical for a workforce in need of highly specialized retraining required to run technologically based systems and processes. While the training for a technician to run or to repair robotic equipment is

> IN THE RECENT PAST, WHEN WORK WAS BORING, ALIENATING, AND DEHUMANIZING, PEOPLE LOOKED TO BUY HAPPINESS OFF THE SHELF. NOW THEY LOOK TO CREATE A NEW FUTURE WHERE THEY CAN CONTROL THE WORK THEY DO AND IN WHICH THEY FIND FULFILLMENT.

extensive, it creates systems that require only a handful of workers. In many industries educational needs shift to generalized liberal education that produces strong problem solving and clear communication abilities and favors lifelong learners willing to embrace fluid work environments. Those who are most successful in the current economy are those who are adept at anticipating the problems, the trends, the technologies, and the needs of the future. As Bill Drayton, CEO of Ashoka, where I am a senior fellow, discusses, new human skills and human dynamic structures are emerging from the era of automation, such that people will work in teams and teams of teams on projects.[65] Moreover, a multicultural workforce will demand that employees across all sectors must be empathetic and embrace diversity to be successful.

This shift to a new economy has been rapid, one fueled by emergent technology and networks. In the process it has fully exposed a gaping digital divide. More clearly than ever before, those who have had limited opportunity to access or learn material stored digitally have been left behind. The pace of how this divide has opened is nothing short of breathtaking. Most historians, particularly when considering the history of England and France, date the first Industrial Revolution as the eighty years from 1760 to 1840. Nearly halving that time, the second Industrial Revolution, often viewed as spanning the years 1870 to 1914, was powered primarily by rapid application of electricity and early use of the internal combustion engine and featured new communications, the use of interchangeable parts, and the emergence of global markets. Similarly, the Digital Revolution— that movement from mechanical and analog electronics to digital

---

65 William F. Meehan III and Kim Starkey Jonker, "Team of Teams: An Emerging Organizational Model," *Forbes*, May 30, 2018, https://www.forbes.com/sites/meehanjonker/2018/05/30/team-of-teams-an-emerging-organizational-model/?sh=112da5236e79.

ones—took, perhaps, forty years, depending on how you measure it, with roots in advancements that accompanied the end of World War II. The Internet Revolution took less than eighteen years from inception to near dominance. The dramatic shift to a remote workforce forced upon us by a global pandemic took less than eighteen months. Each of these dramatic shifts, most notably the latter one, is an example of *capitalism responding to a market problem.*

What Happens Next?

I have little doubt that, as I write this book, we are in the midst of the so-called great reset. The upheaval brought on by the COVID-19 pandemic will undoubtedly create potentially further widening of opportunity for knowledge workers who literally can work from anywhere and lower-skilled workers who have to be physically on the job. This divide is realigning the demographics of the nation, for in many instances knowledge workers, so long as they have internet connectivity, are no longer bound geographically to a location. For those with money, places deemed as "desirable" are experiencing unprecedented growth and inflated housing markets. Those with stable work that can be completed in remote teams often cite lifestyle as the reason for relocation as they seek safe places with good schools. For those without such options, we continue to see an economy that requires them to work multiple jobs to stay afloat, and even those are going away rapidly. Entry-level jobs of the past may not exist in the future. With escalating housing prices, low-income members of our communities continue to be locked out of homeownership with frightening regularity, leaving them to face the precariousness of landlord whims and market pricing. The gap between the wealthy, the shrinking middle class, and the working poor continues to widen. This gap is seen strikingly in the couple of thousand billionaires around the world who can simply live off their investments; their fortunes increased by

54 percent during the first year of the pandemic, according to analysis by the Institute for Policy Studies, while other research organizations place their gains even higher.[66]

The finance sector has not been immune to cultural shifts, workforce demands, and technological advancement. Like nearly all those in knowledge-based industries, CRF relied on a remote workforce during the pandemic, and like all businesses we continue to assess and adjust our needs for physical office space. While the networks required to support remote work are not without significant cost, they are a fraction of the expense to own or lease physical facilities. We made other COVID-19 adaptations as well, particularly in our internal communications and those with our clients and partners.

Large-scale changes in workforce, processes, and markets have clearly been accelerated by the problems encountered and the lessons learned during COVID-19, but much of the changing direction of markets was already happening. Cash-dependent consumers face more new challenges as we move closer and closer to a cashless society. One of my own experiences during the COVID-19 pandemic was a common one but revealing. Quite early in the pandemic, when we were all uncertain what the presence of the virus might mean in our lives, I visited an ATM and retrieved cash. Applying the patterns of the past, I thought that in the face of uncertainty, it might be wise to have money on hand. The reality is that two years later I still carry most of my original cash withdrawal around in my wallet. The currency in my wallet was ancient, and the currency I actually used was digital.

And what is digital currency (and here I am not talking about cryptocurrency)? It's all bytes, ones and zeros flying across the

---

66   Aimee Picchi, "Billionaires Got 54% Richer during Pandemic, Sparking Calls for 'Wealth Tax,'" CBS News, Money Watch, March 31, 2021, https://www.cbsnews.com/news/billionaire-wealth-covid-pandemic-12-trillion-jeff-bezos-wealth-tax/.

internet. I haven't received a physical check from my employer for nearly two decades, yet I manage a huge number of financial transactions, including every monthly bill I pay for utilities, my car, and other recurrent expenses, without ever touching physical currency and most often without even touching a device, for payments from my mortgage to my newspaper subscription are automated. Are the bits and bytes of my pay and my bills real? Rather like that unused cash in my wallet, as a society we have *agreed* that they are real, and we have taken pains to protect and regulate them. Recalling Alfred North Whitehead, we've long moved past mistaking what is concrete for what is abstract, unless of course I tear a bill in half in front of an audience. Yet conceptually the bits and bytes all work, right? Or, more to the point, a digital monetary system works until it doesn't.

On the side of the digital divide where we are comfortable with and have access to technology, we have come to take digital financial transactions for granted. I set up automatic deposits with my employer. I establish automatic withdrawals for my bills. If I am a careful manager of my money, I track my finances and make sure my accounts are balanced, although I suspect I may be in a minority on that front. I can do it all from my computer and my password-protected home router. I can sign legal documents and contracts virtually. As COVID-19 proved, I could process a loan remotely. This all assumes I have access to digital technology and either enough familiarity with it or enough education that I can learn it quickly to utilize it with confidence.

While the more literal parts of the digital divide—lack of access—are quite real and extremely problematic, let's step back a moment first and talk about the divide behind the divide: divisions of wealth, opportunity, education, fair pay, and ownership of assets. Let's continue the above digital list a step or two further. If I have the financial freedom to trade on the open markets, I can do that from a laptop or phone while sipping a latte. Or I can pay a financial advisor to apply his or her expertise and "manage" my money and investments. But first recall that for many Americans the very word "investment" holds little meaning. In 2021 56 percent of Americans reported owning stocks. That number jumps to 64 percent for White adults and drops to 29 percent for Hispanic adults. Polling from the same year reveals that ownership drops to 33 percent for those without college degrees and to 24 percent for those making less than $40,000 a year.[67]

These statistics are only relevant if we assume people have room in their finances to invest at all, a thought that bears a reminder that the personal savings rate (defined as the ratio of money saved by individuals or families to their income after taxes) in 2019, before the pandemic and all of the government intervention applied to offset recession fears, was 7.5 percent.[68]

When you examine data on wealth and asset ownership from the U.S. Census Bureau, the wealth divide looks more like a chasm. The median net worth for the lowest quintile of the U.S. population was $6,030 versus $104,700 for the third quintile and $608,900 for the highest.[69] Breaking down the wealth gap by race is even more revealing. Data from the 2020 census reveal that 28.6 percent of Black people and 18.7 percent of races of Hispanic origin had zero or negative net worth compared with 12.8 percent of Whites. The other end of the spectrum follows suit, with 29.9 percent of non-Hispanic

---

67   Lydia Saad and Jeffrey M. Jones, "What Percentage of Americans Owns Stock?" Gallup, May 12, 2022, https://news.gallup.com/poll/266807/percentage-americans-owns-stock.aspx.

68   Statista, "Personal Saving Rate in the United States from 1960 to 2021," https://www.statista.com/statistics/246234/personal-savings-rate-in-the-united-states/.

69   United States Census Bureau, "Wealth, Asset Ownership, & Debt of Households Detailed Tables: 2019," https://www.census.gov/data/tables/2019/demo/wealth/wealth-asset-ownership.html.

White individuals having a net worth of $500,000 or more, outdone only by Asian individuals (33.1 percent), and quadrupling the rate for Black individuals (7.4 percent).[70] Given that, across all quintiles, the single largest asset most people own is their home, we can't be surprised that Black people and other minorities lag far behind Whites in homeownership rates as well, as this chart from the Federal Reserve Bank of St. Louis makes clear:[71]

HOMEOWNERSHIP RATES BY RACE AND ETHNICITY

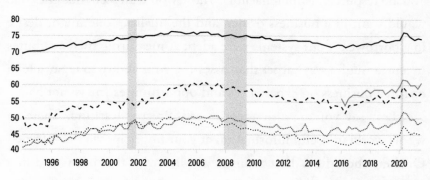

— Non-Hispanic White Alone in the United States
— All Other Races: Asian, Native Hawaiian & Pacific Islander Alone in the United States
– – All Other Races: Total in the United States
······ Hispanic (of Any Race) in the United States
····· Black Alone in the United States

Shaded areas indicate U.S. Recessions   Source: U.S. Census Bureau / fred.stlouisfed.org

If you are unable to afford to own a home, what are the odds that you are able to own a business? That's true even when individuals possess the skills required to be successful business owners. Assume for a moment that you are an entrepreneur who lives in a low-income urban area or in an extremely rural place. You know your community,

---

understand its people *and* its conditions as a market. It's the place you have known all your life. You have a great business idea. But have you received the kind of education that has taught you how to develop a business plan? Do you have access to financial experts? To mentors? To marketers? Assume you have a small margin of equity in your home. Is that enough to launch your business? If so, are you willing to risk your home? How do you find investors when your friends and neighbors are in similar situations? How do you even learn how to reach a wider network of other finance options? What opportunities have you had to work alongside other successful business owners?

You are smart and possess common sense and a desire to learn. You are resourceful and tenacious. Those would all seem qualities one would want in a business owner, and the qualities one might desire in a borrower, if our systems were adept at measuring such attributes in a meaningful way rather than assessing your ability to repay a loan or run a business on experiences and opportunities you've not had.

Let's say you are also adept at self-directed learning. There's a whole world of useful information at your fingertips via the internet. Or there should be. That assumes you live with the means and in a place where you can have reliable access to it. Or that you can navigate government websites if you do have access. Or that you have a way of knowing there might be a breed of bankers different than those you associate with the kinds of banks with household names who would be willing to consider your business idea seriously.

In order to maximize chances of success in this country at this time, one must have an extraordinary array of things most people do not have. This is a massive missed opportunity. Rye Barcott coined the phrase "talent is universal; opportunity is not" when referring to inequitable opportunity in the developing world, but truthfully this axiom applies to the United States as much as anywhere else.[72]

So what of those who fall on the other side of the digital divide? For those still dependent on cash transactions, what happens when the rest of the world moves away from cash? How does a culture react when that notion that has been so ingrained in us disappears, when those physical pieces of paper to which we have attributed value are no longer used? How often have you encountered a restaurant or other business that no longer accepts cash? Much of the European Union has been considered a cashless society for most of the current century; surely the U.S. is not far from cash transactions becoming near anomalies. As this transition occurs, we ask many to move abruptly to an acceptance of misplaced concreteness when they may not have the access to the tools necessary to do so. In November of 2021, the Federal Communications Commission estimated that more than twenty-one million people in the United States don't have consistent access to the internet. According to the Pew Research Center, that "includes nearly three in ten people—twenty-seven percent—who live in such rural places as the outreaches of Maine and the fertile fields of Indiana, as well as two percent of those living in cities."[73]

For some, not participating in the digital economy may be purposeful, for they may be skeptical of or unfamiliar with online tools. They may be unbanked and using money stores or stored value cards purchased at discount retailers, actions that put them further and further behind in building the credit financial institutions expect. But for many, they are on the wrong side of the digital

---

72 Frederick and Barbara Erb Institute, University of Michigan, "At the 2012 Clinton Global Initiative University: 'Talent Is Universal: Opportunity Is Not,'" April 5, 2012, https://erb.umich.edu/2012/04/05/at-the-2012-clinton-global-initiative-university-talent-is-universal-opportunity-is-not/.

73 Joyce Winslow, "America's Digital Divide," Pew *Trust Magazine*, July 26, 2019, https://www.pewtrusts.org/en/trust/archive/summer-2019/americas-digital-divide.

divide simply because of where they live, because they cannot afford the hardware necessary to access digital transactions, or because they either don't have or don't know how to use the limited public access points available. Meanwhile, we are speaking of entire industries, like internet providers where we privatize profits but socialize costs and most typically governmental entities foot the bill for infrastructure development. While the marketplace has often largely left such people behind, in this moment it feels especially acute. As markets begin to move toward even greater use of technology, more and more fintech enterprise takes root, and society moves toward a larger embrace of things like cryptocurrency, who wins and who loses?

We are in a period of a rapidly shifting economy. If you are on the wrong side of the digital divide, you really are not able to prevail in the changing tides. In part this is an infrastructure problem. The 27 percent of Americans without consistent broadband access would benefit greatly from federal government action on infrastructure spending or corporate commitment to creating a system accessible to all. The broadband system is not going to build itself, nor evidently are those in the industry who provide internet service. Without such infrastructure, the hurdle for many is extremely high, and given the networked, digitalized nature of the finance industry, it is truly a hurdle we must overcome. Fortunately, Congress has passed an infrastructure bill and the Inflation Reduction Act, both of which contain funding to address the digital divide as well as the climate emergency.

Yet that is only part of the "divide" equation.

Let's say one of our business owners in the above scenario defies the odds, finds someone to invest in their idea, and successfully opens a business. If it is a Black entrepreneur we have imagined, it's still going to be an uphill battle, and success may remain measured. For starters the Black entrepreneur will likely have more debt. Start-up capital is associated with better business performance, but Black entrepreneurs generally have less of a track record due to the systemic challenges outlined in previous chapters. Black entrepreneurs start their businesses with about $35,000 of capital, White entrepreneurs with $107,000. As a partial consequence, Black-owned businesses report higher levels of debt relative to revenues.[74] The majority (63.9 percent) of all new businesses, regardless of race or gender, utilize personal savings or financial support from their families for start-up capital. Overall, bank loans account for 17.9 percent of start-up capital, and 10.3 percent use personal credit cards. Black business owners are outliers on these total percentages, relying more than any other group on credit cards for capitalization and least on bank loans.[75] Moreover, most Black-owned businesses remain small both in number of employees and in revenue generated. They also face market barriers resulting from unaddressed needs related to challenges of access—to capital, expertise, and services. Equally important, they encounter sociocultural barriers that can block them from gaining social capital, such as helpful relationships that make up business networks. A report from McKinsey and Company reveals how location can be an additional barrier:

> Sixty-five percent of Black Americans live in sixteen states that are below the US average on indicators of economic opportunity. Within their communities, Black Americans are also disproportionately concentrated in economically dis-

---

74 David Baboolall et al., "Building Supportive Ecosystems for Black-Owned US Businesses," McKinsey Institute for Black Economic Mobility, October 29, 2020, https://www.mckinsey.com/industries/public-and-social-sector/our-insights/building-supportive-ecosystems-for-black-owned-us-businesses.

75 Tiffany Howard, "The State of Black Entrepreneurship in America: Evaluating the Relationship between Immigration and Minority Business Ownership," Congressional Black Caucus Foundation, Center for Policy Research and Analysis, April 2019, https://www.cbcfinc.org/wp-content/uploads/2019/05/CPAR-Report-Black-Entrepreneurship-in-America.pdf.

advantaged neighborhoods. Black entrepreneurs from these communities are less likely than their white peers to have exposure and access to lucrative business opportunities.[76]

As if that weren't all enough to stack the deck, a uniting force comes along—COVID-19. There is direct linkage between minority business ownership and the shifting markets experienced in the COVID-19 era, and we are wise to assume a post-COVID-19 world in which those who already face stiff challenges to access the tools that can lead to successful business ownership will be challenged once again. "Black business owners have been disproportionately affected by the pandemic-linked economic downturn, partly because they were more likely to already be in a precarious position, including more likely to be located in com-

DESPITE HAVING MADE GAINS IN THE DECADE PRECEDING THE PANDEMIC DUE AT LEAST IN PART TO INCREASING PUBLIC AWARENESS ABOUT WEALTH INEQUALITY AND FROM FOCUSED INTERVENTION FROM THE CDFI INDUSTRY, COVID THREATENS TO UNDO THEM.

munities with business environments that are more likely to produce poor business outcomes."[77] Other minority- and women-owned businesses have experienced similar difficulties. In a national survey conducted by the Stanford Latino Entrepreneurship Initiative, they found that "Latinos have fewer resources to weather the ongoing storm. Latino-owned businesses have less cash on hand and when requesting funding from the Paycheck Protection Program, Latinos have their PPP loans approved at half the rate of white-owned businesses. An even

---

76   Baboolall et al., "Building Supportive Ecosystems."

77   Baboolall et al., "Building Supportive Ecosystems."

smaller proportion of Latino-owned businesses gets their full funding relative to white owned-businesses."[78]

Sadly, this comes just after a time that had begun to produce some hope of change. In a painful irony, nationally, minority- and women-owned business enterprises "added 1.8 million jobs from 2007 to 2012, while firms owned by white males lost 800,000 jobs, and firms equally owned by white men and women lost another 1.6 million jobs,"[79] yet minority- and women only–owned enterprises were more likely to go out of business during the Great Recession. Despite having made gains in the decade preceding the pandemic due at least in part to increasing public awareness about wealth inequality and from focused intervention from the CDFI industry, COVID threatens to undo them. Early data suggest that we may see a repeat of the Great Recession's unequal impact again with losses during the pandemic.[80] Add to these dilemmas the reality that many minority-owned businesses concentrate disproportionately in medical services, restaurants, and small-sector retail—growth can be difficult, and profits are often slim. Many of the industries in which minority wealth is focused bore the brunt of permanent or temporary closures during COVID-19, and many suffered permanent staff departures. Couple the number of employees fleeing sectors like food service with the larger loss of entry-level positions because of automation and other forces as we have examined, and recovery for many minority- and women-owned businesses will be challenging.

---

78   Marlene Orozcolnara et al., "The Ongoing Impact of COVID-19 on Latino-Owned Businesses," Stanford Latino Entrepreneurship Initiative, August 2020, https://www.gsb.stanford.edu/faculty-research/publications/ongoing-impact-covid-19-latino-owned-businesses.

79   Sifan Liu and Joseph Parilla, "Businesses Owned by Women and Minorities Have Grown. Will COVID-19 Undo That?" Brookings Institute, April 14, 2020, https://www.brookings.edu/research/businesses-owned-by-women-and-minorities-have-grown-will-covid-19-undo-that/.

80   Liu and Parilla, "Businesses Owned."

The COVID-19 pandemic revealed drastic inefficiencies in what have proven to be fragile value chains. Border closures and lockdowns disrupted production and transportation and contributed to an 8 percent drop in trade in 2020—the biggest since the global financial crisis.[81] The reasons behind global supply chain disruptions are complex and multifaceted, but most economists and trade experts predict that they will last long after the pandemic ends. Because we live and participate in a truly global economy, these disruptions impact everyone, but as with all crises, those who suffer the greatest tend to be those who are already the most vulnerable. That reality is particularly visible in the countries with the least financial wealth, but it also disproportionately impacts minority communities in the U.S. Similarities to the unbalanced access to social infrastructures made minorities, especially Black Americans, suffer far greater hospitalization and death rates in the first year of the pandemic, with higher numbers at the low end of the wealth gap. More dependent on service industry and manufacturing jobs, they will suffer the impact of supply chain disruptions more keenly as well. As supply chain issues shifted from handcuffing sectors like computer chip manufacturers, impacting the production of everything from cars to appliances to shortages of food and petroleum products, folks with lower incomes were disproportionately affected. These sorts of disruptions, particularly in agriculture and maritime transport of goods, will only worsen with the accelerating impact of climate change, where, once again, the economically vulnerable become more vulnerable. Potentially worsening the impact of supply chain concerns is that politicization, where far-right conservatives are more likely to deny climate change

---

81   Paul Brenton et al., "Stronger Value Chains, Not Reshoring, Are Needed after the COVID-19 Shock," World Bank Blog, March 3, 2022, https://blogs.worldbank.org/trade/stronger-value-chains-not-reshoring-are-needed-after-covid-19-shock.

and dismiss the severity of the wealth gap, tend also to argue in favor of reshoring manufacturing. Others counter that detangling the complexities of the global supply chain is not only impossible, but that attempts to do so could be harmful, indeed, and, perhaps ironically, they suggest that it is the free market that can supply the best solutions via reducing trade barriers and further integrating global value chains by doing more to bring developing nations more concretely into the world economy. Congressional legislation as sweeping as the Inflation Reduction Act and as targeted as shoring up the semiconductor industry passed in the summer of 2022 may help on these fronts, but more ambitious progress with faster mandates on implementation of alternative fuels and the like are required to address the severity of the problem. Reports presented by the World Bank suggest that a shift toward global reshoring to high-income countries and China could drive an additional fifty-two million people into extreme poverty, most of them in sub-Saharan Africa, whereas better integration of developed and developing countries in order to increase resilience to market shocks could lift almost twenty-two million people out of poverty by 2030.[82]

NETWORKS, THE INTERNET OF THINGS, AND EMERGENT FINANCIAL TECHNOLOGIES

Sadly, just as businesses owned by women and minorities tend to face greater difficulty accessing financial and social capital, they are also underrepresented in the technology sector and are far less likely to have opportunities to participate in emergent trends like the Internet of Things (IoT). The world has fully entered the network age, a reality that will change everything in a post-COVID-19 climate: networks of

---

82   Brenton et al., "Stronger Value Chains."

people, networks of cyber "realities," networks of information storage, networks of economies, and networks of things. Economies have become interactive with advancements in technology and changes in communications structures. At the same time that many people have become less connected in their real, physical communities, they are increasingly connected in remote, digital networks. These patterns go against the historical grain of minority communities and rural places, where, particularly in poor communities, the ability to know and depend upon neighbors and extended families has often been central to economic survival. Think for example of the importance something like a locally owned barbershop has in a Black neighborhood or a small-town coffee shop has in a farming community as places not just of commerce but of socialization and informal community information exchange. What will replace such community institutions? If they are lost, what else will disappear with them? Can social media really make up such a gap? If you lack financial resources and don't live in close proximity to an extended family, how do you afford childcare? For reasons far beyond the physical reality of connectivity required to participate in the digital landscape, such communities are not well positioned to enter into many aspects of networked social lives, let alone networked markets.

If you have doubts about the transformative power of the current marketplace to upend small businesses or indeed entire industries, I challenge you to think about just a few of your own daily commerce exchanges and then ask questions of them in a new light. How greatly has the rate of deliveries of packages to your home increased in the past decade? When is the last time you physically saw your doctor? How many of your daily functions are managed by apps accessed through your phone? When is the last time you entered a bank for cash? When did you last enter a florist shop? Are you old enough to remember a thing called a map (and yes, I'm talking about something that's not on your phone)? Do you have a network-connected doorbell or thermostat?

How many streaming services do you subscribe to? Today we might be hopping from one service to the next to chase our favorite programming, but we've long ago lost sight of what these streaming services replaced: once-thriving video stores, whether they were operated by a corporation like Blockbuster or of the mom-and-pop variety. By the start of the pandemic, streaming services filled the void created by mandatory lockdowns and stay-at-home entertainment, but now we must ask, will movie theaters rebound, or will they go the way of video stores?

Central to rapid changes that disproportionately impact those the CDFI sector serves with greatest frequency include our rapid movement to a cashless society. When is the last time you wrote a check? How often do you use cash? How we pay for goods and services is upending a lot of small businesses. Recently, I was in Miami and my family and I entered a restaurant where we encountered a big sign declaring that it was a cashless business and that all transactions needed to be completed using a credit card or digital wallet. Upon seeing the sign, my immediate thoughts were twofold: 1) if you don't have credit, you can't eat there regardless of your ability to afford a meal, and 2) if you are a practicing Muslim, because interest is forbidden in Islam, you can't have a credit card. The technology might be useful for the business, but it excludes some customers, and thus a facet of the modern marketplace can make cultural and technological shifts inadvertently discriminatory.

If you are like most of us, the most frequent visitor to your front door works for a variety of delivery services, whether that is a package carrier bringing you goods you purchased online or a driver delivering your dinner. We are all aware of the juggernaut of corporations the size of Amazon and the impact it has on small businesses. What we might give less thought to is the degree to which e-commerce also cuts out a lot of middlemen. This latter phenomenon has a similar effect of removing income from small businesses. For Amazon the movement from its founding to becoming the world's most valuable retailer took just twenty-one years.

The network represented by the IoT may provide the clearest example of the systemic change I'm talking about with the above examples, for in the most literal sense we are creating interconnected networks of devices that can share information and "speak" to one another. One example above, the power of the map that's on your phone, has not only made it unnecessary for you to learn almost anything about your surroundings, but it is also already linked with your web browser, your Yelp app, your public transit system, the gig driver who has replaced your taxi driver, your app for tracking physical exercise … it's a rather simple example about the power of networks and interconnected information.

Of course, it requires economic freedom to participate in the fullest benefits of the IoT, and it requires full access to digital technology. Fully joining the IoT will require substantial change, in mindset and in technology, for all of us in the global marketplace, but it is a particular threat to those left behind who have less wealth, education, access to vibrant networks, and technological savvy. Overwhelmingly, the industries that can apply the full power of the digital age are owned by fewer and fewer people. That makes the challenge of bringing more people into markets additionally challenging. The implications to daily life are sizable. The implications for nearly any viable business model are greater still.

The IoT is a byproduct of larger connected electronic networks that are akin to the highways and power grid of the old industrial economy. It's part of why companies can provide twenty-four-hour service as customer requests are transferred from one time zone to another without customers being aware that the work is being done on the other side of the world. It is how they can manage their purchasing, invoicing, document exchange, and logistics through global networks that connect a billion computing devices. Of course, it takes scale and sophistication to accomplish such tasks. This is so true that there will no doubt either be a movement in which large corporations take further control of nearly every sector or small businesses will have to become more integrated into their own networks to compete. Just as robber barons emerged from the industrial age and the household names who run the Big Five of the tech sector have guided economics and policy in this fledgling century, the IoT will forever alter markets.

Change of massive scale comes rapidly in today's market. Its pace will only accelerate. Even those enterprises with billion-dollar budgets have failed to predict the shape of this post-COVID-19 economy again and again. Can small businesses keep up? Can they predict the changes on the horizon and adapt their business models? Can small businesses that already face massive competitive hurdles stay relevant? When we're thinking about trying to build intergenerational wealth in the BIPOC community where there is, as I have discussed, a need for and a natural appetite for service businesses that feature a lot of entry-level jobs, the kinds of inexorable changes in a modernizing, technology-driven marketplace demand that small businesses become extremely innovative or they will get crushed by huge conglomerates. If it is hard for big business to adapt to shifting markets, it can be nearly impossible for small entrepreneurs.

What history has shown us with consistency is that those with the least opportunity to participate in markets always suffer the most in times of transition. Among the slowest to benefit from the industrial age were farmworkers. And who were/are farmworkers if not overwhelmingly Black and Brown people? Where did electrification reach last? Low-income communities and the most rural parts of the country. Who has been left behind in everything from readily accessible quality nutritional options to health insurance plans to internet access? The same people who struggle to find affordable housing options and procure business loans. We cannot speak about a vast network like the IoT without also addressing the parallel movement toward networks of humans and shifting needs in the workforce.

> *WHAT HISTORY HAS SHOWN US WITH CONSISTENCY IS THAT THOSE WITH THE LEAST OPPORTUNITY TO PARTICIPATE IN MARKETS ALWAYS SUFFER THE MOST IN TIMES OF TRANSITION.*

In the midst of a market shift led by automation that will impact everything from displacement of workers to needed reeducation, the community development industry is facing complex new challenges, some of which have their genesis in similar shifts in technology and mobile applications but also have emerged from entities looking to find pathways around regulators amid an evolution of global finance.

I do not have the knowledge to analyze all the market implications and complications that cryptocurrencies create, but it is worth taking just a moment to highlight the potential larger implications of the technology that makes digital currencies possible. Blockchain is a technology, not a corporate entity or a consortium of users. Whether in finance or elsewhere, it is so potent a technology and so related to the larger concept of networking that its applications will necessarily grow. There is little doubt that blockchain technology will soon be used in medical records and in all sorts of noncurrency commercial applications; for example, there are already insurance companies that use blockchain technology to issue instantaneous travel refunds for ticketed airline passengers who have their flights delayed or canceled. There is absolutely no doubt that blockchain technology, like internet technology before it, will fundamentally alter markets in myriad ways. Blockchain technology has certainly entered the mainstream, and the currency it created maybe can be viewed as having done so as well. While I don't profess to know enough about cryptocurrencies to make more specific pronouncements about their future or to predict how regulators will attempt to manage their existence, I do believe it is vital for all of us in the financial sector to better educate ourselves about them. What I do know it that crypto markets will be volatile, will be subject to market forces, and will require regulatory oversight just as surely as any other capital market.

By strict definition cryptocurrency is part of the larger fintech, or financial technology, market. "Fintech" is the term used to describe any technology that delivers financial services through software. Fintech includes online banking and mobile apps. It encompasses many different technologies, but the primary objectives are to change the way consumers and businesses access their finances and compete with traditional financial services. Traditional banks have used fintech for decades. Perhaps the best known nontraditional fintech company, PayPal, was established in 1998. Other big players arrived later: Venmo in 2009 and Zelle in 2017. It seems entirely likely that technology companies, most notably Meta, will one day operate the world's largest banks, even if they call them something different.

But much of what we think of as fintech today includes an entire cast of characters that didn't exist before the late 1990s and several of which challenge the expectations of traditional banks. With the 2008 global financial crisis, many people lost their trust in traditional banking, and millennials in particular welcomed free and online financial services. Those technologies have now evolved and given birth to payment apps like Apple Pay and Google Pay, crowdsourcing like Kickstarter and GoFundMe, robo-advisors that use algorithms to make portfolio recommendations, stock trading apps, and insurtech companies.

Some would argue that fintech companies have made financial transactions become more convenient, efficient, and accessible, in part because they are flexible and fast when it comes to implementing new services based on changing demands. There is no doubt that they are disrupters in the financial sector and have taken market share from traditional banks. Fintech executives would certainly tell you that they can deliver on social change and can reach people who were disadvantaged by traditional banking services. When it comes to payment services, that may be somewhat true. But when it comes to fintech advances into banking services like loans, credit cards, and personal credit lines, I would argue that many have preyed upon historically underinvested and underbanked communities by not being transparent about their approved credit rates and focusing on high returns. This is possible because of unlevel regulatory environments between online fintech companies and traditional banks. Federal regulators in the U.S. and around the world have been slow to keep pace with their rapid evolutions and growth. As I argued early on in the book, capitalism without controls always creates upheavals that then require market adjustments, many of which come in the form of regulation. I have little doubt that we are headed for a similar upheaval in fintech, particularly if corporate giants like large tech companies continue to see opportunities to move deeper into the financial sector. We have already proven that as a society we have been poor predictors of the power of tech companies to alter media and politics, so why should we be surprised that they may forever alter finance in similar ways? It might be worth keeping in mind that one of the three founders of PayPal was Peter Thiel, the first outside investor in Facebook, and that early in its history PayPal merged with a fintech founded by Elon Musk. It is significant that some of the largest players in fintech really are tech companies accustomed to the world of start-up ideologies and venture capital, not in the greatly regulated environment of traditional financial institutions. There's a lot we can't know about the fintech future. But what we have seen throughout human history is our species' capacity to act on greed. As a result we have witnessed repeated examples of how those with the greatest abilities and opportunities to act upon their greed end up excluding others from the systems they create to accumulate wealth.

In a culture where the distance between those who have and those who have not is not only growing but is doing so in familiar patterns that discriminate from those who are seen as "different" or as outsiders, history does not suggest that accelerating movements like fintech and blockchain technology bode well for people with low incomes or for people of color. While we have other technologies, like cellular devices, that could allow mobile financial apps to close gaps for those we have previously excluded, I wonder if we have the moral fortitude to use them to such benefit. Certainly, that will not be the case unless corporate leaders inside and outside the financial industry take actions to use new technologies as a means to create inclusive capitalism. In a post-COVID-19 market, the need for morally responsible, mission-driven leaders will be greater than ever before.

The post-COVID-19 marketplace, like the awakening to the pluralistic culture that today defines the demographic make-up of the United States, is hampered by a number of "gaps," foremost, as I have discussed at length, the income gap. I have explored others as well, such as the digital divide and the gap of credit history and physical proximity to financial services. Yet of all the gaps that divide people in our current culture, the one we most have to address is the gap of trust. For much of the history of this country, many in low-income communities have distrusted financial institutions and, by extension, those who work in them. Such distrust is born out of experience and is not unlike the distrust many people of color have for law enforcement. Until we provide people on the fringes of capital markets a reason to believe that the financial sector is capable of wide-scale change, the most innovative programs our best thinkers can dream up will not be enough. So how do we change? How do we meet the challenges the last two chapters have exposed? That's what I will address next.

CHAPTER 8

SHOWING THE WORLD IT CAN BE DONE

The highlight of my career has been the thirty-five years that CRF has repeatedly proven that financial innovation can be successful. At numerous turns in our history, we have had to create or adapt financial instruments in order to maintain our mission. We have demonstrated our belief in taking calculated risks, been open to the unexpected, and displayed unwavering commitment to solving the problems that affect the communities we serve, and we have consistently illustrated the kind of agility that makes me confident we can continue to be industry leaders in changing post-COVID-19 markets.

As I have tried to make clear over the last two chapters, American markets, and indeed American culture, are at a unique inflection point, one where the products, services, and innovations we and others in the CDFI industry have developed will continue to expand in the mainstream capital marketplace, where demand will grow, and where we can be uniquely positioned to help transform people's lives for the better. To accomplish those aims requires that we continue to innovate. That has been the ongoing CRF story: evolving new approaches, adapting to new market conditions and regulations, developing new products, and bringing new technologies to the industry. We have consistently shown the financial industry that there are ways to expand its reach and bring new faces into the success story of American capitalism.

The challenges we encountered in the past were significant. So are those on the horizon. While there is trending interest in ESG investments, it has not yet entered the mainstream fully. The very nature of financial markets is constantly undergoing changes—sometimes sweeping, more often incremental—for investment mindsets shift with new technologies, new opportunities, changing consumer sentiment, and changing political and social interests. In order to change the trajectory of income growth and opportunity and build on trends that nudge interest in ESG into broader markets, multiple challenges—in housing, education, safety, workforce, and health—must be solved concurrently, with an eye toward holistic, sustainable change instead of quick fixes. In order to illustrate that inspired, driven people brought together by a common mission to help others can enable better access to capital for more people and catalyze financial ecosystems, this chapter will highlight some of the most innovative solutions I've been fortunate to help apply through CRF. It is from the kinds of mission-driven innovations this chapter elucidates that we will find future tools that can expand our reach and deepen our impact as we face challenges—new and old alike.

> **WE HAVE CONSISTENTLY SHOWN THE FINANCIAL INDUSTRY THAT THERE ARE WAYS TO EXPAND ITS REACH AND BRING NEW FACES INTO THE SUCCESS STORY OF AMERICAN CAPITALISM.**

FOUNDATIONS IN INNOVATION

What are the building blocks that support creating scalable, equitable opportunities for underserved people to access capital? The early history of CRF detailing the significant hurdles we encountered in getting the company off the ground is instructive not only about the terrain in which today's ESG trends trace their origins but also about the nature of how social enterprises operate and how they can make inroads within established systems. It is also instructional about how we might continue to move activism from our streets to our boardrooms.

CRF is one of a number of successful CDFIs that have been on the leading edge of innovation. In 1988 when we founded CRF, people didn't think about socially minded entities as credible investment opportunities. Yet the groundwork for change had begun nearly two decades before because of the creation of Fannie Mae and Freddie Mac. Their development created liquidity in housing markets by purchasing loans and forming opportunities for people to invest in the bonds and notes issued through the federal home mortgage market. Seeing such programs and others as models, a handful of people were beginning to think that nonprofits could become capital velocity vehicles. In our case Warren Hanson and I began to identify a number of revolving loan funds, mostly tiny efforts meant to fund community programs or affordable housing development. We identified more than three hundred such revolving funds in Minnesota that were interested in making investments outside of where banks were lending. Alone, these funds didn't really have the capital capacity to scale solutions in proportion to challenges small businesses were facing. We understood the problem these funds faced, so we developed a policy framework and persuaded the legislature to authorize cities and economic development agencies to sell loans without going through a public bidding process.

CRF came into being as a market maker for the loans that emerged from our public policy efforts, which simultaneously allowed us to relieve the burdens the state encountered in holding community-minded loans to term. Knowing of the work I had been doing in Minnesota state government, where my career first focused on housing and then on energy, Terry Saario, who was then the CEO of the Northwest Area Foundation, took me out to lunch one day and told me, "We know that you and Warren have been working on this concept, and we are interested in funding it, but we don't fund the state. We're willing to help you start a nonprofit if you're interested." Once I retrieved my jaw from the floor, I saw what she was proposing as a unique opportunity. I jumped ship from my job with the state into the unknown world of nonprofit social enterprise.

The Northwest Area Foundation is one of the legacy foundations of the James J. Hill family and the Great Northern Railroad and was started by James's son, Louis W. Hill. The region served by the foundation—Minnesota, Iowa, North Dakota, South Dakota, Montana, Idaho, Washington, and Oregon, as well as the seventy-six Native nations that share the same geography—corresponds to the freight routes of the Great Northern Railway. About the time that Terry approached me, its board had recently changed its focus to increase giving in economic and community development in low-income areas and particularly on Native American reservations throughout its service area.

The first steps of CRF are instructive for the future as well, for they demonstrate how novel ideas and new approaches can be difficult for regulators—and potential investors—to understand. The newly formed CRF faced a first step of proving to the IRS that we should be approved as a charity under Section 501(c)(3) of the Internal Revenue Code. As a charity CRF would not be required to pay income taxes, and more importantly, donors to CRF would be able to take a deduction on their federal taxes. The challenge was showing the IRS that we were indeed a nonprofit, albeit one that applied quite a unique model. Another aspect of the process of seeking determination as a 501(c)(3) public charity was that CRF was not a private foundation, which would subject donations from other private foundations to an excessive excise tax. The code provided several ways in which an entity could avoid being deemed a private foundation. We chose to become a "supporting organiza-tion," and we ended up supporting a class of other nonprofit and governmental lenders with a dual role of community development and economic development with a charitable purpose. We were not a typical nonprofit seeking charitable donations from the public, but a highly specialized nonprofit that, at the time, was quite confusing to the IRS. While we built on experience developed within community development corporations, this was long before the creation of the CDFI Fund at the Treasury Department or formal declaration of the CDFI designation. That would not arrive until 1994 when the Riegle Community Development and Regulatory Improvement Act of 1991 was signed into law. No one had really done what we were attempting to do before. If we are to solve the problems of creating greater inclusion in the financial industry, we are going to need many more "never-attempted-before" ideas.

Any organization that wants to be able to deduct charitable con-tributions from its taxes has to do so through a 501(c)(3) organization that has received a determination letter from the IRS acknowledging its approved charitable status. Generally, the IRS acts within ninety days on these applications and issues what is called a determination letter granting tax-exempt status under 501(c)(3). Ninety days came and went, and we heard nothing from the IRS. During the interim, while we sought approval from the IRS, CRF operated as a program of the Minneapolis Foundation, which served as a fiscal agent for our start-up activities. The Northwest Area Foundation made its first donation to the Minneapolis Foundation, a vital community foundation authorized to receive tax-deductible contributions from other funders. The Minneapolis Foundation wrote the checks and verified that what we were doing was consistent with a charitable purpose. We paid them a fee for being our fiscal agent. The initial funding from the Northwest Area Foundation was sized to cover the initial months of operation until we had our determination letter and could begin raising contributions from other funders.

For months the IRS was silent, and I began inquiring about what was taking so long. We needed money from the grant to establish an office and hire a staff. Every day that we didn't receive our approval was a day in which more money drained from our account at the Minneapolis Foundation. Entities interested in the investment interests we had proposed began to slip away. We had, for example, successfully courted Honeywell to garner its support, but when it saw that we didn't have any money, it temporarily withdrew its interest. We dearly needed such a partner to make it through the IRS delay. Finally, after a frustrating exchange with the IRS in Chicago, I learned that the complexity of our application caused it to be sent to the IRS in Washington, DC, and that office was not bound to any time limit for making its determination. From here I have to recognize the extraordinary privilege and good fortune CRF received to be fully launched. I was connected to Minnesota's U.S. Senator Dave Durenberger and Congressman Martin Sabo, whom I exasperatedly asked to intervene on our behalf, not to pressure the IRS for a favorable decision, but to pressure them to *make* a decision. Finally, things started moving, but, to our dismay, the IRS denied CRF's request for recognition as a nonprofit, and we wondered if our idea was dead before we had ever even started. We felt the status was legitimate if only we could help them understand what we were proposing, so we appealed their ruling. So began an instructive if extraordinarily frustrating period in the "history" of CRF. Can you have a history before you formally exist?

As Christmas neared, with all the financial institutions that we needed to talk to closed for the holidays and without a letter in hand from the IRS that would allow us to solicit donations, the well had run dry. I was able to pay the staff. On Christmas Eve I wrote myself a check for zero dollars as a lesson to remind me that I would never let this sort of circumstance happen again. It was one of the most depressing times in my life. I went home that night and talked with my wife. With her encouragement our family wrote a check to the Minneapolis Foundation to keep CRF afloat for another month. It was a wing and a prayer at that point.

An early believer in our mission, Norwest Bank (the predecessor to Wells Fargo) stepped up to help us pay for the IRS appeals process. Thankfully, the appeal was turned around in a week. The ninety days the IRS had initially promised ultimately took eleven months. With the arrival of the official IRS determination after the holiday season, we were able to begin securing grants and start the wheels turning on the waterfall security investment structure we had developed. CRF would never have happened if it weren't for people like Terry Saario and Karl Stauber and the Northwest Area Foundation, and Jon Campbell at Norwest Bank, and others who believed in our vision.

What are some of the takeaways from CRF's bumpy history if we are to solve the problems of the future? We need original ideas and thoughtful experiments; new ideas require tenacity to be implemented; we will always work inside existing systems of markets and market regulators and must be innovative in meeting their requirements; it takes networks of people to support even the best ideas; we must so believe in our mission that we are willing to give it the whole of ourselves.

VALUE NETWORKS

The foundation involvement had proven something that I'd believed from the beginning—that success revolved around a public/private/philanthropic partnership, forming what is commonly referred to as a value network. In the 1980s there wasn't yet much of a public component, but we were convinced that we could find foundational capital among philanthropists. In an era well before most foundations had begun to think in terms of what we now label mission-related investing and focused on conservative grant disbursements within their untaxed limits, we began to help them see that there could be methods to leverage their balance sheets without sizable risk exposure and thereby exponentially increase their impact.

The public sector simply wasn't ready to get involved yet, and we had to find a lot of unconventional capital just to prove we could accomplish our objectives and then a great deal of follow-on capital once we did. Perhaps it was hubris on my part, but for a long, long time I wanted CRF to run without any state or federal money. I simply did not want us to become another supplicant at the federal trough. We eventually were able to get some seed money from a state appropriation that would match philanthropic money, my one and only instance in those early days of using public money. We were greatly aided by the willingness of Mike Dougherty, managing director at

Dougherty, Dawkins, Strand and Yost, a boutique investment bank, with whom I had worked when at the state. His associate, Tom Peterson, took a real career risk by bringing an unknown nonprofit into the firm, but they agreed to be the placement agent on our first debt securitization. Bruce Bonjour, an outstanding bond attorney with whom I had also worked at the state, provided us ideas and expertise on how to structure a deal. He offered to provide his services pro bono until CRF was up and operating. These acts of kindness and support were instrumental in launching CRF.

By investing philanthropic capital inside the structure, we were able to build a platform where, if the underlying loans didn't perform, those buying the bonds would still be able to recoup their money. The theory was to reduce risk and in return to attract massive amounts of private capital to the community development space. The approach we developed was so novel that it took a while to purchase loans, but ultimately we were able to secure loans from two nonprofits and three public agencies. Similarly, investors took their time as well. Our first deal was small, somewhere around $2 million, and unusual in that, because we didn't have a lot of capital, we had to get all five loan sellers, including the Crookston EDA, to sign on before we could close the bond issue. But once we did, they delivered their loans, we placed them into a grantor trust, sold the bonds, and were off and running.

> **THE WORK OF SOCIAL ENTERPRISES NEVER HAPPENS IN A VACUUM; IT REQUIRES SIGNIFICANT PARTNERSHIPS.**

Based on the proof of concept that we could successfully put together this innovative financial instrument, the Northwest Area Foundation cut us a check for $1 million, and from their involvement we were able to approach the McKnight Foundation, which was the largest foundation in Minnesota. Because the leadership team of these two foundations believed in us, we were able to begin to "turn the flywheel," as it were, and prove to others that the approach we were taking could work. Their presence brought others to the table, and over the course of the 1990s, we were able to develop more securitization instruments for larger and larger bond issues. The development of such an innovation is what I now can look back on and see as the first phase of proof of concept. It also offered a lesson from which we have never strayed: the work of social enterprises never happens in a vacuum; it requires significant partnerships.

ATTRACTING MAINSTREAM INVESTORS

As thrilled as we were in our initial issues, we knew that what we had created were still essentially boutique securities. To attract more investors and expand the impact of what we were attempting, we knew that we needed to achieve a rating status for the securities from one of the recognized debt-rating agencies. There was no secondary market for such securities at the time, and investors had to hold the bonds to maturity, so it was difficult to get accredited entities to see the stability of these devices.

Our cause was helped by some unique occurrences taking place inside the larger financial industry. This was the era of banking consolidation. Interstate commerce laws had changed, allowing banks to begin expansion beyond what had once been their narrow authorizing charters. The big fish were actively looking for smaller fish to gobble up as they moved across state boundaries. Community- and family-owned banks were targets for purchase in order for regional banks to gain a foothold in new markets. Helpful to our cause was that banks were anxious to be able to demonstrate to regulators that they were following the Community Reinvestment Act and investing in low-income census tracts. In 1989 such desire to demonstrate good faith was provided new incentive as a revision to the CRA put teeth into its objectives. The Financial Institution Reform and Recovery Act of 1989 (FIRREA) included an amendment to CRA statutes requiring public disclosure of institutions' ratings and performance evaluations. FIRREA also expanded data collection and made public certain data. With the requisite data becoming available, advocacy groups, researchers, and other analysts began to perform more-sophisticated, quantitative analyses of bank records and evaluate if they were meeting the credit needs of the communities where they did business.

Another shift that assisted us was an extension of the CRA rules that defined securities that were "innovative and complex." The Office of the Comptroller of the Currency within the Treasury Department issued CRF a letter confirming that our securities fell into the innovative and complex category. That in turn allowed federal regulators to acknowledge the legitimacy of what we were doing. All of these factors working together gave us greater ability not only to help influence ongoing federal policy but also to nudge the dial forward with foundations to increase their mission-related investing. At the time, Luther Ragin (a future CRF board member) was the chief investment officer at the FB Heron Foundation. He became a vital advocate for foundations investing their corpus in their mission in order to elevate their social impact. FB Heron became an early partner, and its presence, along with others, continued to open doors.

With foundations and other philanthropies expanding their role in generating grants, we were better positioned to go after the "brass ring" so essential to expanding the kinds of investors interested in the security vehicles we had developed. That meant positioning our products so that the ratings agencies could evaluate their soundness.

In the early to mid-1990s, the cause of social enterprises in the financial space was greatly aided when the Federal Reserve Bank of San Francisco, then under the leadership of Janet Yellen, focused a great deal of attention on the concept of community development investing. Their activity included the formation of an advisory board, of which I was invited to be a member, and the development of a journal dedicated to the field, all aimed at helping banks understand the concept of community development investments. Under the leadership of a focused team at the San Francisco Fed led by David Erickson and some simultaneous scholarship by Michael Swack, a professor at the University of Southern New Hampshire and now leading the Center for Impact Investing at the Carsey School at the University of New Hampshire, what once were laissez-faire community investment networks became formalized. Swack created the Financial Innovations Roundtable, which brought together a number of thought leaders focused on the work of CDFIs.

Around this same time, Greg Stanton formed an organization he called Wall Street Without Walls, which was focused on connecting capital market institutions and financial products with organizations engaged in community economic development in low- and moderate-income communities. Greg was an icon on Wall Street, having securitized the future royalties of David Bowie's entire music portfolio. He understood financial innovation, and he saw the promise in the CRF model. Between Swack's and Stanton's efforts, they were able to get representatives of the major ratings agencies to participate in discussions about community development as an expanding market. Building on the success of CRF note issuances, we engaged the firm of Jackson Securities, the firm founded by former Atlanta mayor and civil rights leader Maynard Jackson, to help us refine the structure of our bond issues. Jackson personally led our efforts to move CRF securities to the next level. I will never forget the day that he spent with me personally enlisting Atlanta corporations and foundations to support CRF and our vision. He even took me by the house where he was born to a mother who sang opera. Sadly, Maynard died not long after and never saw the results of the time he spent with me that day and the impact he and his firm had on guiding CRF.

Applying a great deal of innovation, partners, and advocates like these I have mentioned and many, many others began to create mechanisms for the rating agencies to adapt models that allowed them to analyze sufficient data and provide ratings to the security tools we had developed. Once we were able to demonstrate that our products had received AAA bond status, we were able to attract a far greater diversity of investors. That in turn allowed us to enhance the scale and volume of the securitizations we issued.

What had once seemed novel or even outlier approaches to increasing the impact of social investments became a creditworthy, proven approach, and as we continued to develop standardized products, we were able to profoundly increase our social impact.

REPEATING SUCCESS IN THE FACE OF SKEPTICISM AND STRESS

At the beginning stages of CRF, repeatedly we encountered people who said, "You can't do that. It's just too difficult. It will never work." And time and again we replied, "We're going to figure it out. We'll show the world that it can be done."

Community development corporations were some of the few survivors of President Johnson's Great Society initiatives and of reorganization that took place during President Reagan's administration. In the early and mid-1990s, several of these organizations had come together to experiment with a pilot program called the Community Development Tax Credit Coalition with the aim to incent private investment in community development corporations.

During this time we were extremely fortunate to have nurtured a vital relationship with Bob Rapoza, one of the giants in the world of community development on Capitol Hill. I met Bob when he was representing the National Congress for Community Economic Development, and he invited me to come to a dinner with a group he represented called the Eagles, who were a number of leaders of community development corporations. After conversations with Bob and with the Eagles, I brought CRF into the coalition. One primary objective of the coalition was seeking legislative support for a tax credit to stimulate private investment into community development organizations. We were all greatly aided by the remarkably effective support of Gene Sperling, the director of the National Economic Council.

Throughout the latter half of the 1990s, Bob was relentless in his work lobbying Congress, requesting legislative support for the ideas coming out of coalition discussions. Each year he thought he got a little closer. Hope gained greater footing when President Clinton, on a trip to Chicago, succeeded in getting the speaker of the house, Dennis Hastert, to shake hands and agree he would see that the House took action. Yet by late 1999, as Clinton's term ended, Bob told me, "I think we're going to have to go to the next round," and I put my file on New Markets away. Such a setback didn't seem surprising even if it was disappointing, yet surprise did arrive when Bob abruptly called and said, "Something's moving. We've got to get back to work on this."

Throughout the late 1990s, we had been involved in a coalition seeking to create a tax incentive for investments in community development organizations. Over time the CDC Tax Credit Coalition adopted a larger vision that morphed into the New Markets Tax

Credit Coalition. After years of toil on Capitol Hill by so many in the social enterprise community, the New Markets Tax Credit Program (NMTC) became a reality with the passage of the very last major bill of the Clinton administration, the Community Renewal Tax Relief Act of 2000. President Clinton was deeply interested in what came to be known as "new" domestic markets, for in his travels as president in both dense urban areas and sparce rural ones, he had observed how desperate some low-income communities truly were and was convinced that there needed to be innovative, government-backed, competitive market mechanisms for investing at home. Community development entities apply to the Treasury Department's CDFI Fund to receive tax credit authority. NMTC investors provide capital to community development entities and in exchange are awarded credits against their federal tax obligations. Investors can claim their allotted tax credits in as little as seven years—5 percent of the investment for each of the first three years and 6 percent of the project for the remaining four years—for a total of 39 percent of the NMTC project. A community development entity can be its own investor or find an outside investor. Investors are primarily corporate entities—often large international banks or other regulated financial institutions—but any entity or person is eligible to claim NMTCs. Because I was the president of the New Markets Coalition, I was invited to the White House for the bill signing, which was one of the highlights of my life.

To its credit, the Bush administration honored the law and understood its intent. Much of the accolades for helping the bill not get lost in the bureaucratic shuffle of new administrators during the administrative transition resides with Bob Rapoza. The cost of the program has fluctuated over time, including higher allocations in response to Hurricane Katrina and as a part of the American Recovery and Reinvestment Act, but the NMTC program has held steady at around $1.4

billion per year. Congress authorizes the amount of credit, which the Treasury then allocates to qualified applicants. From 2003 through 2020, the program parceled out credits worth $26 billion (in 2020 dollars). The credits have supported projects in Puerto Rico and in all fifty states, and in recent years all applicants have pledged to place at least 75 percent of their NMTC projects in "severely distressed" census tracts.

At least in my experience, not only is the work of creating these kinds of programs always a long battle requiring innovative thinking and resilience, but the major milestones have also often been accompanied by dramatic events in my own life. That certainly was the case with NMTC. We were sailing in uncharted waters as we tried to implement the law within an administration that had not written it.

TOILING FOR CHANGE

CRF was anxious to participate in NMTC, so we hired Mary Tingerthal, my first boss at the Minnesota Housing Finance Agency and a trusted friend, to be our vice president of capital markets and tasked her with overseeing our application for the first allocation rounds of the program and with forming a lot of new relationships with major Wall Street players. Mary had a stellar career at the National Equity Fund and later as commissioner of Minnesota Housing. She was one of the few people in the country who truly understood the value of the NMTC at the time. We saw the NMTC as a tremendous innovation and wanted to go big, applying for over $200 million.

About the same time, we were contacted by Joe Stark from Bear Stearns. Joe was intrigued with NMTC and with CRF. He took a deep dive into the securitizations we had done in the past, essentially reverse engineering what we had created, and called us and said, "You guys have this totally figured out. It's a huge career risk for me, but I want Bear Stearns to invest with you in NMTC." Our first face-to-face meeting was scheduled for the afternoon of September 11, 2001.

That morning I was booked to have breakfast with Susan Shapiro, with whom I had worked previously on fundraising for community development projects. Susan was in town from New York City. On the drive in to work, *Morning Edition* interrupted itself to announce that a plane had crashed into one of the Twin Towers. By the time I arrived at my breakfast with Susan at the Marquette Hotel inside the IDS Center, the news from New York was escalating. Susan expressed concern, intimate as she was with terrorism given that the judge who was the target of the 1993 truck bombing of the World Trade Center lived on her block and remained under federal protection. Over the course of breakfast, murmurs grew around the dining room, and at one point our server said she could take our coffee to the business center where they had a television set up. After the second plane struck, Susan excused herself and said that she needed to find a way home as soon as possible. On departing she said, "I'll never forget that I was here with you, Frank, when I think of this day." As I exited the hotel and crossed the skyway that connects the IDS Center to the building that housed the CRF offices, I passed a television and saw the south tower of the World Trade Center collapse.

Before the day was over, Joe Stark called and said, "Frank, I'm not going to make our meeting. I'm grounded in Traverse City, Michigan." Eventually, we did meet, and Bear Stearns became an important, large-scale investment partner, yet I cannot think of that period of time and not place it within the context of the 9/11 tragedy. Ironically, after years of trying to build NMTC instruments and more than a year of working with the Bush administration to finalize NMTC's details, time devoted to work that could develop so much good for so many people, in my mind the period leading into its implementation is caught inside such senseless destruction. It was a time of uncertainty and chaos, and it felt like it mirrored much of the period leading into the passage of NMTC and the process of hammering out its working nature.

Because of all that was involved in finalizing the program and the nature of implementing federal programs, ultimately the allocations for 2001 and 2002 were combined. They totaled nearly $2.5 billion. Like the traumatic linkage for me between NMTC and 9/11, the period from passage of the NMTC program to actual allocation offered several personal and professional battles that are central to how I view this period of time, including an unlikely personal incident.

Now I hope I have proven farsighted when it comes to the financial innovations, but when it comes to my literal vision, I am terribly nearsighted. My vision had been bad since childhood, and I finally decided to have a LASIK procedure completed—a detailed process that takes place in a series of steps over several days. During the long wait to see if CRF would be included in the first round of NMTC allocations seemed as good a time as any to undergo the procedure. On a Tuesday in the spring of 2003, I arrived at my ophthalmologist, where they used a microkeratome to create the corneal flap before they reshaped the lens and put the cornea back in place. This was before doctors used lasers for this part of the procedure, and the microkeratome employed a physical blade. There I was, already nervous because someone was cutting my eye (which, of course, I could not help but see), my thoughts and senses dulled by a sedative the doctor had given me, when I heard her say simply, "Uh, Mr. Altman, we're not going to be doing your left eye today." Then after some more probing of my right eye accompanied by her heavy breathing, she explained, "Your flap has not been properly cut. I'm going to have to see you tomorrow." She went on with more explanations that were largely lost on me and then kept repeating that it was vital I keep the eye moist until the following day's appointment, since the procedure causes a temporary decrease in tear production.

Essentially blind in my right eye, I left with steroid eye drops and strict orders to use them. My wife, Leslie, was a judge at the time, and she had to be in court that day. I asked one of my young staff members, Nick Elders, if he could assist me, and when he took me home, recognizing that I was blind and anxious, he stayed with me to make sure I was okay. We took the time to talk about his future at CRF, and we decided that he should focus on technology. That discussion was a crucial event in Nick's career, as now he is CEO of Ignify Technologies, a spin-off from CRF that is streamlining the origination of SBA and other business loans in CDFIs and banks across the country—another moment of brightness emerging from a difficult, uncertain time.

The next day, on Wednesday morning, distracted by my eye and anxious about my afternoon appointment, I was in a meeting when my assistant entered and passed me a sticky note that simply said, "167 and a half million." We had news from the Treasury Department. That was the size of our first NMTC allocation! It was the largest allocation ever made by the CDFI Fund. Approximately half of that allocation was to be used for the deal Joe Stark had facilitated through Bear Stearns. I was thrilled.

That afternoon I returned to my ophthalmologist in high hopes this day would go better than the previous one had. She examined my right eye and told me that it looked good and that she would see me the next day to continue monitoring my recovery. When I had exited my meeting, giddy with the news of our allocation, I had learned that Treasury Secretary John Snow was going to be in Columbus, Ohio, the next day to formally announce the allocations and that CRF was invited to attend. I told my ophthalmologist that I had to fly to Ohio and would need to postpone until Friday. She said, "There's no way you can fly, Mr. Altman. The pressurized air on a plane is far too dry."

"You don't understand," I told her. "This has consumed the last five years of my life."

With some pleading on my part, she finally relented but loaded me up with eye drops, issued repeated warnings about keeping the eye moist, and demanded that I keep my eye closed throughout the flights. Driving home from the appointment, I felt as if something in my eye had moved. The feeling concerned me, and I had a sense of prescient doom, but no outward signs of change occurred. I made my flight the next day, met Treasury Secretary Snow at the announcement ceremony, posed for the requisite pictures, and departed feeling that we had accomplished something remarkable. In the years since that fabled start, the largest allocation the fund has made has been $90 million, and we opened the history of NMTC with $167.5 million. You may wonder where the other half million went. It went to Racine, Wisconsin, and it still stands as the smallest allocation in the history of the credit.

I returned to my doctor on Friday, ready to put the procedure behind me; however, fate decided to offer up a cruel twist. Immediately upon seeing me, my ophthalmologist said, "Mr. Altman, I'm afraid your flap has slipped. Epithelial cells from the outer cornea have migrated under the flap. It's something we need to address immediately." My disappointment at suffering this rare complication was palpable, but then anxiety really set in when she then said, "I'm terribly sorry, but I simply can't complete the correction today. I'm scheduled to move my parents into an assisted-living facility this afternoon. I'm going to arrange to have one of my colleagues fill in for me. He's agreed to meet with you tomorrow for a consultation and determine a course of action. He's excellent at these repairs."

Already daunted, I arrived at my appointment to find the clinic officially closed. The doctor had used a phone book to prop the door open so I could enter. The lights were off. There was no receptionist and no nurse in sight. Eventually I found the doctor, someone I had never met. He took one look at my eye and said, "We're not going to wait on this. We need to do the surgery right now. I don't have a nurse with me, so you're going to have to help." I was too floored to respond intelligently. I wanted to turn tail and run. I had met the treasury secretary, testified before congressional committees, ventured into the uncharted territory of starting a social enterprise without a map, but never could I have imagined serving as my own nurse, with no sedatives, while a cranky and seemingly eccentric stranger performed surgery on my eye!

Once he had his microscope and other equipment set up and me positioned in the chair, he set about attaching the sterile field cloth on my face. Whereas my normal doctor was the epitome of calm and cool, this doctor wore his emotions on his sleeve, and he was slamming drawers open and closed, complaining about nurses and where they kept materials he needed. He could not find a metal contraption that was supposed to hold the sterile sheet away from my nose and mouth so that I could breathe. "I can't find it," he said at last, exasperated. "You'll have to hold it up." He added anesthetic drops to numb my eye, and before he started the procedure, he said, "Now, Mr. Altman, you have to remain perfectly still. You absolutely *cannot* move."

There I was, one arm outstretched, all my being focused on remaining still while the bright light of the microscope seemed to drill into my eye. You cannot imagine the agony it is to command your eye not to blink. Partway through the procedure, my cell phone, which was in my pocket, started to ring. I tried to turn it off with my only available hand. Apparently, I instead pushed the button to answer the call, for I later learned that the call was from Leslie, and she could hear every part of what was happening in the surgical room. Her accidental eavesdropping included the moment when, while placing sutures on the flap, the doctor grumbled loudly, "What the hell is going on here? I've got blood." And it was blood I could see and, worse still, feel, for he had gotten the third suture into the white portion of my eye, which does not absorb anesthetic drops. The pain was excruciating, yet I was intent to do as commanded and not flinch.

By the culmination of the procedure, my eye looked like it had been through a meat grinder, much as I felt during the hurry-up-and-wait maneuvering required throughout the five years of working to make NMTC a reality. Given the depth of CRF's immersion in attaining our allocation, I felt emotionally bonded to NMTC. The personal travails of a normally minor elective surgery feel oddly fitting to the stress I felt in this period as NMTC moved from a thought exercise to reality. But more importantly, I am continually reminded that my personally stressful experience of this time remains incomparable to the injustice and daily suffering of the people who stand the most to gain from such policy instruments. Yet the work was so worth it. Through fiscal year 2020, $55.9 billion in new markets tax credits have been

> **I AM CONTINUALLY REMINDED THAT MY PERSONALLY STRESSFUL EXPERIENCE OF THIS TIME REMAINS INCOMPARABLE TO THE INJUSTICE AND DAILY SUFFERING OF THE PEOPLE WHO STAND THE MOST TO GAIN FROM SUCH POLICY INSTRUMENTS.**

invested in low-income communities since the program's inception.[83] When I look back on that very first, record-setting allocation made to CRF, the stress fades away when I think of the three hundred or more businesses we funded across low-income communities around the nation.

We were able to use NMTC and a new partnership with New York City's Robin Hood Foundation as a guarantor to take on a project as sizable and as impactful as building a charter high school in the Bronx. The KIPP New York City College Preparatory High School in the South Bronx is a prime example of how the right investment can become transformative for a whole community. Serving a part of New York City that is disproportionately home to kids from financially disadvantaged families, this school boasts a 97 percent graduation rate that sees 46 percent of its matriculated students graduate college.[84]

ADAPTATION AND INNOVATION

The nearly universal fear, frequent despair, and all-too-regular ruin suffered with the financial markets collapse in 2008 and 2009 brought renewed reminders of both the stress the work in the CDFI industry can instill and the real harm that our sector is trying to rectify. I have already detailed the CRF experience of the Great Recession, but after so many years of laboring inventively and intensely to demonstrate to the world that we could produce meaningful change, market conditions forced us to pivot and recalibrate financial tools for new times yet again.

---

83   The CDFI Fund, *NMTC Program Award Book, CY 2020*, https://www.cdfifund.gov/sites/cdfi/files/2021-08/CY2020_NMTC_Program_Award_Book_FINAL.pdf.

84   KIPP NYC: Public Schools, "Our Results," https://kippnyc.org/results/.

Because of the success of NMTC and the use of securitization instruments like CRF developed, CDFIs had become something equivalent to the *Good Housekeeping* seal for a lot of investors. Despite the high regard with which many investors held CDFIs, with the 2008 collapse, the reactive shock meant that CDFIs, like financial institutions of far greater size, had no new deals to cut. Credit had dried up. As investors grew highly conservative, outside of our continued involvement in NMTC for high-dollar projects, we had to move to doing single-investor, single-project finance in order to survive.

Throughout CRF's history we have worked with Congress and others to develop policy initiatives that can increase the impact of CDFIs, yet ironically, CRF did not actually become a certified CDFI until 2009. To act on our need to pivot, the first step was applying for official certification as a CDFI. From there, we saw new immediate avenues forward: by moving into single-project deals using NMTC allocations, by becoming a Small Business Administration (SBA) lender through the acquisition of a national nonbank SBA 7(a) license, and by building on our relationships with other CDFIs and creating deeper, networked cooperatives to develop efficiencies and increase the scale of our collective impact.

It had become quite clear that if we wanted to continue to access the capital markets, we needed to have a trusted resource to de-risk our financial instruments, and there was no more trusted resource than the SBA, a federal agency that has the full faith and credit backstop of the federal government. SBA was a decades-old lending platform but one that was not really available to the borrowers that CDFIs serve in general. In fact CRF was only the second CDFI in the nation to receive a national nonbank SBA license. The first recipient was the National Development Council through its Grow America Fund. As pioneers in mission-driven SBA lending, it offered us a great deal of wisdom and direction for how we could accomplish the greatest good through the platform.

The SBA relies primarily on bank regulators to oversee safety and soundness, but it did issue a certain number of licenses to nonbank lenders. But by 2009, determining that they did not have sufficient staff to make certain all such entities were fully compliant, they decided to cap the number of nonbank licenses at fourteen. (Recently the SBA announced that it would lift the cap on the number of national nonbank 7(a) licenses it would supervise. Given the track records of CRF, NDC, and more recently LISC as nonprofit stewards of these licenses, I hope that the SBA will grant approval to more CDFIs serving hard-to-reach communities.) Those licenses became like twentieth-century taxi medallions in New York City because at the time they would trade for tens of millions of dollars such that only enormous companies could typically afford them. However, CRF got lucky. One of these licenses had been purchased by a private equity firm, but its parent company had filed for bankruptcy, and this license was essentially "orphaned." What had been a $20 million license was potentially available at a fraction of the cost. We were able to get the FB Heron Foundation to assist us with a grant in order to acquire the license, which maintained our ability to continue lending and keep accessing the capital markets in the postcrash credit desert. There had been a flight to quality by investors (you may recall that there was a period after the crash when interest rates on treasury bonds went negative), and the SBA secondary market was part of their destination. Fortuitously, during this same period, the SBA wanted to act on its growing awareness that it was not effectively reaching people of color. Getting SBA support for the license took real effort and a fair amount of hoop jumping because we obviously did not have direct SBA lending experience, but we did have an outstanding track record, one that had proven our ability to reach women- and minority-owned businesses in particular, filling a market the SBA desperately wanted to serve better.

While CRF has funded literally hundreds of small businesses around the nation in the years since becoming a preferred SBA lender, simple examples from our own hometown, like the story of Karibu Deli I shared earlier or the support of Arubah Emotional Health Services, capture a sense of how we have been able to assist under-invested communities. With three locations throughout the Twin Cities, Black- and woman-owned Arubah Emotional Health Services provides outpatient mental health counseling to people living and working in low-income neighborhoods. Patients come to Arubah for cognitive behavioral therapy as well as evidence-based therapies such as art, yoga, and hypnotherapy. CRF assisted Arubah in its purchase of a new location in North Minneapolis that would serve as a fourth service location as well as a business headquarters. This is but one example out of hundreds, but Arubah Emotional Health Services demonstrates the kind of trust-based, community-focused investment that can literally transform, perhaps even save, lives.

While one of our points of pride prior to 2008 was an ability to make smaller business loans of the half-million-dollar variety similar to Arubah, the costs of NMTC compliance force deals to be quite large, bottoming at $5 million to $7 million. By becoming a qualified Small Business Administration lender, we were still able to serve those businesses that only had capacity for smaller projects. Additionally, we have partnered on larger transactions with other CDFIs, creating business loan conduits. Through multi-CDFI partnerships, we have been able to assist in making loans to both urban and rural distressed communities, from funding small, Black-owned businesses in the heart of Harlem to a firefighting facility on the Hoopa Reservation in northern California, from financing a lithium-ion battery manufacturer in the Pacific Northwest to helping fund redevelopment of downtown Grundy, Virginia, in the heart of coal country to move it out of a flood plain.

NEW OPPORTUNITIES REQUIRE NEW TOOLS

We began making SBA loans in 2011, and as we embarked on this newest aspect of our evolution, we knew that as an organization, we wanted to be technology forward from the very beginning. Our own reality at the time was that we were still stuck in what I call the sneaker network. Most of our file storage and documentation was still on discs, requiring us literally to walk loan files from computer to computer. Our expertise remained in software spreadsheets, and much of our credit processes involved cutting and pasting material into files, so the ability to maintain integrity and compliance was compromised. I have always believed that it is not efficient to throw people at a problem that technology can solve. I recognized that properly applied technology in the finance world, just like in other industries, creates efficiencies that also assist in the development of the networked approach we sought.

To that end the needs of the SBA program created the perfect opportunity to expand our use of technology. We initiated a survey of existing software platforms that could support SBA loan originations. We discovered that a number of them were still using DOS-based systems. Because we did not want to try to adapt legacy software that really couldn't do what we wanted, we decided to build our own system that would include the ability to identify and track community impact, which most other lenders don't care about. What we created was SPARK, now a powerful cloud-based origination software for SBA and other small-business loans.

After 2008 the other bit of happenchance alignment that advantaged our position arrived through a federal pilot program that was developed out of lobbying efforts called Community Advantage that gave CDFIs the right to make SBA 7(a) loans that were distinct from traditional SBA requirements and allowed for lower business credit scores. It required participating CDFIs to take on more risk, but they also could charge higher fees on the theory they would make a lot of small loans that are otherwise inefficient. While CRF was not eligible for the program because by then we already had our SBA license, we saw that SPARK could be an ideal loan-origination system for the program and began making it available to other CDFIs. The giving arm of one of Walmart's companies, Sam's Club, became really interested in building the capacity of CDFIs and funded much of our early development of SPARK and our efforts to broaden its use by financial institutions for mission-driven work. Later on the MasterCard Center for Inclusive Growth became another vital financial backer. Today not only is SPARK used by a number of CDFIs, but scores of other SBA preferred lenders, particularly community banks, also employ it.

SPARK, alongside other technological efficiencies we have developed, is an excellent example of showing the world what can be done. It has been analyzed by consultants and regulators and is widely viewed as best in class in the marketplace, particularly its ability to be configured quickly so that institutions adopting it don't have to spend a lot of time or money with consultants during installation. Because it is a product that excels at meeting the specific needs of SBA loans, it already contained a lot of the critical apparatus required when we needed the agility to move rapidly into the Paycheck Protection Program (PPP). Not only could we utilize SPARK for this new application, but CRF is also unusual among CDFIs because it has met all the criteria necessary to be a preferred SBA lender, allowing us to have a direct connection to the SBA, something very few lenders have. SPARK is not the only platform through which institutions can complete PPP loan origination, but its quality and robust nature certainly gave us and other adoptees a significant leg up in meeting the high volume of demand.

It is partially through the development and forward thinking associated with software like SPARK and other technology platforms that positioned CRF to become a market leader. To best serve consumers in the post-COVID-19 era, our sector must address how we build on the true value proposition of smaller CDFIs: their ability to establish cultural competencies and trust in communities where there is frequent mistrust of banks. While CDFIs are viewed as trusted partners among those that use them, they produce little loan volume. That is a vital imbalance. The vision that we've always had at CRF is to knit together a network that demonstrates the strength of a large-scale, efficient operation but that supports local organizations in ways that enable them to accomplish the essential missions they perform. Many of the smaller CDFIs are raising more than half of their operating dollars from grants, which leaves very little money that can go out on the street once they have met their operational expenses. They don't have easy access to technology that can support them. By creating networks of CDFIs that can share resources and infrastructure, we facilitate their dollars to have greater reach. CRF's latest effort at accomplishing a shared utility has been in aggregated lead demand and impact reporting. Through a tool called Connect-2Capital, CDFIs are able to list loan product parameters, and loan seekers are able to complete a simple preapplication to "match" with an appropriate provider and product. Providers underwrite loans (using

SPARK or other systems), and outcomes for borrowers are carefully tracked. These data can be disaggregated by race, gender, industry, credit score, and more to understand outcomes for different kinds of borrowers. I like to think of such networks as modeled by businesses like Ace Hardware or Carpet One, linking together thousands of independently owned enterprises, thus reducing their costs of supply procurement by being able to produce collective volume. The more we implement such models in finance, the more we can create environments where CDFIs can continue to be the face of customer services and interaction with their borrowers, but ones where a lot of the back-office operational functions can be done at scale at a lower cost per unit.

SAME SONG, DIFFERENT VERSE

Over the course of my career, I have encountered an anxiety-based unfamiliarity with the core approaches CRF has taken that I have had to dispel time and time again. At each roadblock CRF encountered, our past experience made us confident that we understood the market tools that would make what we were attempting possible. We just had to convince potential partners and investors of two things: why it would work and why it fulfilled the kind of missions to which they were committed.

I share these stories of CRF's shaky infancy and challenging growing years not only to underscore how new our concepts were with each stage of our development, but also to reinforce how often social enterprises are forced to prove the effectiveness of their concepts. By nature social enterprises challenge the status quo. Social enterprises regularly require resiliency, reinvention, and innovation. Social innovation, whether charitable or for profit, takes grit and determination.

CRF has nearly thirty-five years of experience applying innovative financial tools. We have consistently restructured and revised CRF as market conditions and cultural shifts have demanded. It is valuable and rewarding work, and I take pride in what we have accomplished. We have, time and again, proven what can be accomplished when we stay mission-focused but remain open to ideas and approaches that many consider unconventional. Indeed, what is lacking is not will or ability or convention but scale. How do we expand the impact of CRF and other mission-driven financial institutions as we move forward into an uncertain future? That is the subject of the final chapter.

CHAPTER 9

A VISION OF WHAT CAN BE

You no doubt remember the story of my rather dramatic experience with LASIK surgery. Permit me to use one aspect of that story as a metaphor. One of the most common conditions LASIK is intended to correct, as in my case, is myopia, or what is colloquially referred to as nearsightedness. One can reasonably argue that what has kept American capitalism from maximizing its benefits for the greatest number of its citizens has been, in part, caused by myopic thinking. Too often our vision of capitalism has been to generate maximum financial return with little foresight into the future or into the potential repercussions. It is, for example, simply easier to believe the risks of planetwide fossil fuel consumption will not create consequences in our own lifetime when our portfolio that includes equity shares in nonrenewable energy companies has grown exponentially with each passing quarter. If we could know with precision that the effects of actions we were participating in today would risk the lives of our children tomorrow, I suspect we would change our behaviors. We are also all typically guilty of the myopia involved when restricting our vision to the impacts of decisions on ourselves and on those in our immediate orbit. If George Floyd were our family member (or looked like someone who could be), we would be neither impartial to nor dismissive of his death.

We are all guilty of myopia even when we wish we were not. Those few prognosticators who regularly warned that policy and behavior would result in the economic collapse we now label as the Great Recession were not only in a microscopic minority, but they were also viewed as outliers. Several scientists and public health officials have been writing for decades about the likelihood of a global pandemic but were either dismissed or ignored. There always seems to be something more pressing, doesn't there? I hope that you may exit this book seeing not only that the issues I have focused my attention

> THE ISSUES I HAVE FOCUSED MY ATTENTION UPON ARE PRESSING—URGENT, IN FACT—BUT ... WE ALREADY HAVE MANY OF THE TOOLS IN PLACE TO MAKE POSITIVE CHANGE HAPPEN. WHAT WE TEND TO LACK IS THE WILL AND THE VISION FOR WHY WE MUST CREATE CHANGE.

upon *are* pressing—urgent, in fact—but that we already have many of the tools in place to make positive change happen. What we tend to lack is the will and the vision for why we must create change. Such nearsightedness simply cannot stand.

I ended the last chapter with this question: How do we expand the impact of mission-driven financial institutions as we move forward into an uncertain future? Inherent in the question is part of its answer, for we must create far greater *scale* in the CDFI industry. We must make the products and services offered by CDFIs—for investors and for those seeking capital—more widely available and more readily accessible. That need is what is behind CRF's willingness to join into networks that link multiple CDFIs on large deals, in our success in meeting the stringent requirements that allow us to operate in multiple states, and in the purposeful manner we have applied when developing unique instruments like Detroit Home Mortgage, SPARK, and Connect2Capital. Such initiatives and cooperative ventures suggest examples of commonsense approaches that enlist available innovation and that challenge narrow perceptions of capitalism. To reduce the disparities that have minimized economic mobility among historically underserved populations requires better tools, more partnerships, stronger networks, and more innovation. As I close this book, I wish to identify very specific needs of financial social enterprises in the immediate future and suggest action-oriented mechanisms to expand their impact. At the same time, I wish to propose ways that the growing appeal of ESG investing can take advantage of current trends in capitalism and on the expanded vision of inclusion felt by a majority of Americans, particularly among younger people.[85]

The proposals that I believe are needed require urgent action. The racial wealth gap continues to widen despite greater awareness among the general public about the human consequences of its presence. The clarion call that accompanied George Floyd's murder risks fading into the din of the twenty-four-hour news cycle and America's proclivity for forgetfulness. The economy of the post-COVID-19 era is tumultuous and unpredictable and will prove slow to correct course given the entangled fragilities that have been exposed in global markets and just-in-time inventory strategies. A seismic shift of attitude toward expectations about work, happiness, and sustainability has accompanied market instability. Yet here are plenty of smart, creative, caring

---

85 Paradigm, "Nearly 7 in 10 Americans Think Racial Injustice Is a Problem, and Believe They Should Be Able to Talk About It at Work," May 19, 2021, https://www.paradigmiq.com/2021/05/19/nearly-7-in-10-americans-think-racial-injustice-is-problem-and-believe-they-should-be-able-to-talk-about-it-at-work/.

professionals in the CDFI industry who recognize that the status quo cannot stand and who have the experience and have developed the tools that can make change happen. There simply are not enough of them. Our portion of the larger financial industry must grow if we are to address the needs laid bare in 2020 by the pandemic and renewed demands for social justice. As the last chapter detailed, those immersed in financial social ventures aimed at inclusion have established methodologies for altering the course of an imbalanced system, but to reach the scale required will require immediate action from private, public, and philanthropic sectors working in harmony.

We stand at a nexus of need and opportunity. Need will not disappear, while opportunity very well might. Most certainly the unique opportunities of the current moment will vanish if we continue to suffer the prolonged absence of political will to expand capitalism's reach and if policymakers continue to craft rules and regulations intent on protecting those who have already amassed wealth. If we cannot scale the products and services offered by CDFIs and other community development entities, we simply cannot shrink the wealth gap. A failure to do so mires the poorest among us in conditions that should be an embarrassment for the wealthiest nation on the planet and holds quite serious consequences for the future of capitalism and, potentially, for the future of our democracy.

The reality of our current macroeconomic state in the U.S. is a mixed bag and extraordinarily complex. We have made notable advancements. Certainly, the efforts of ESG investing have moved the needle forward for those long locked out of access to capital. But the reach of the wealth gap is far. Americans, particularly people of color who fall below the poverty level, are imperiled by systemic and multigenerational cultural realities with twin roots in economics and culture. The result for these folks has included higher levels of chronic medical conditions; poor access to quality education, nutrition, and job diversity; lower life expectancy; and more exposure to hazardous environmental dangers. Such factors combine with other realities I have detailed in previous chapters that work in a complex web of interrelated deficits that tend to keep poor people poor. And in the presence of poverty, other literally deadly consequences arise, whether in the form of heat sinks in the urban core of cities where most people with low incomes live or in the lack of diverse work opportunities that make upward economic movement nearly impossible.

Complicating matters more is the linkage between the "E" and the "S" and "G" of ESG investment, for when we begin to study climate justice, we quickly recognize that the same people who have historically been locked out of business development and homeownership have also suffered the most direct impacts of global climate change, air and water pollution, and other environmental factors that worsen health, shorten lives, force migration, and sustain poverty. This book has barely touched on the impacts of climate justice, but the communities on which we in the CDFI industry focus our work tend to live either in urban centers or small rural places; they are also the ones more likely to live in urban heat islands, flood zones, farm and rangeland undergoing desertification, in close proximity to abandoned factory centers, and near EPA cleanup sites. Environmental degradation and financial hardship become double-edged weapons. Climate justice and social justice are inextricably linked. The window of opportunity for positive change in both arenas may be narrowing and will require recognizing their linkage, creating ever-more innovative approaches to solutions, and continuing to build both advocacy and public-relations efforts. The 2022 passage of the Inflation Reduction Act is a very positive step, but we must use it as a launchpad for greater action, and we should not be placated that it alone resolves the substantial problems I have outlined or that it represents a sea change. I am thrilled with the bill's passage, its impacts on global climate change, and its improvement of healthcare access for low-income Americans; however, it arrived at a time when counterforces indicate that a battle for change is far from won.

Because denials and delays from the far right regarding human causation of climate change (notably often the same political force most intent on securing a status quo vision of capitalism based on trickle-down economics) further stall urgently needed policy change, the immediate future for the communities we serve appears bleaker still. When the Supreme Court made its ruling in *Citizens United v. FEC* in 2010, it completely changed the landscape of campaigning and elections. By allowing corporations and outside groups to spend unlimited amounts of money on electoral campaigns, the decision altered our mechanisms of accountability, making an already out-of-balance system worse. Politicians have become beholden to their biggest donors, rather than pursuing the policies demanded by the people. That decision has harshly eroded congressional will to take action to address climate change. Every day of delay for implementing requirements to reduce dependence on fossil fuels has life-and-death consequences. That Supreme Court ruling, coupled with the June 2022 decision in *West Virginia v. EPA*, which sharply confines the Environmental Protection Agency's ability to regulate carbon emissions from power plants, is indicative of the current gap between policy and essential environmental sustainability and risks hamstringing the federal government's ability to create or regulate environmental policy that might address the urgency of needed response to the climate crisis. In contrast with the position taken by the court, the centralized leadership role of federal rules and regulations is required if we are to mitigate our current deadly trajectory in regard to the impacts of climate change. Just as I have taken pains to demonstrate that regulated markets are vital to reduce the destructive effects of potential market failures, history offers ample evidence that those intent on maximizing profits are willing to do so despite harm to human and planetary health absent reasoned, thoughtful regulation. The potential repercussions of the *West Virginia v. EPA* decision, since it questions the essential ability of federal agencies to develop or enforce regulations, will likely have severe regulatory impacts on the financial industry as well, providing further roadblocks to the actions we so desperately need to take. The politicization of these issues, which is perhaps most boldface in efforts by some conservatives to block even simple requirements for financial institutions and corporations from making ESG data public, threatens to extend the harm felt by those who are the most frequent victims of both climate change and inaccessibility to capital markets.

CDFIs should be seen as part of the resilience against global catastrophes. What we know with certainty is the future will create more political and climate refugees as water and food shortages become more common and places become uninhabitable. As climate refugees fleeing crisis are displaced, many of them will seek what they hope to be new opportunities, whether displaced

> *CDFIS SHOULD BE SEEN AS PART OF THE RESILIENCE AGAINST GLOBAL CATASTROPHES.*

within the U.S. or arriving from abroad as new immigrants, and their journeys will most often place them in the very communities where CDFIs work with the greatest frequency. Those communities will become more dense and more diverse. These new arrivals will need the assistance CDFIs can provide more desperately than any other group. They, like the rural migrants seeking work in cities and like immigrants and children of immigrants of the past century, will become our neighbors. They will live in the same communities as so many still fighting daily against the multigenerational impacts of poverty, bigotry, and slavery. CDFIs need to be enablers of their resilience, whether through small-business loans, financing for community facilities, affordable housing, or more. We need to provide them a safety net as they work to join an economy that raises higher hurdles for those with the least means.

There remain good reasons for heralding the U.S. as a country where people can rise through economic ranks, but too often we hold out exceptional examples and fail to acknowledge that such exceptions are not illustrative of the norm. Gaining meaningful wealth or, for that matter, simply ascending to lifestyles that offer stability, health, and economic freedom of choice requires equal opportunities for financial access, job growth, and education. I have taken great pains in the lead-up to this chapter to offer evidence that not only are opportunities not equal for all, but there are also systematic forces that remain in place that eradicate opportunity. CDFIs can be a counterforce to such systemic bias. Now is the moment to build on past success and expand our reach. As such, CDFIs have an important role to aid in education about the need for legislation that supports our efforts in the public, private, and philanthropic sectors.

BLENDED INVESTMENTS

In 2017 I attended a meeting at the Economic Innovation Group, the leading advocate for the Trump administration's Opportunity Zones tax provision. However, one of the participants in the meeting noted that he had spoken with a client about the possibility of using the Opportunity Zone provisions to shelter capital gains, and he was met with the response, "So you want me to sell my Apple stock and invest in a war zone?" My unvoiced but desired response would have been, "Well, yes, I'd like you to replace at least some of your Apple stock with this investment." I hope by this point I don't have to explain the inherent elitism and potential racism revealed in his remark. But in fact my desire that he target at least some of his investing into ESG-focused enterprise is an important part of the overall need for the future. Community development and investment works exist across a spectrum of for-profit investment and philanthropy (and, since 2000, government backing through new markets tax credits and other means). Before I offer some specific prescriptive actions I would like to see in each of the three sectors, let me first address a few broader needs that have applications for the blend of public, private, and philanthropic social enterprises.

We need to find ways for people to actualize where they want to invest. The growing use of ESG scores for banks, companies, and stocks is an important first step, but investors who wish to support social enterprises would benefit from education on ESG ratings. We would also benefit from better metrics for measuring social impact. At present most ESG scores come through MSCI, a company with expertise in research, data, and technology. While MSCI does an excellent job offering quite comprehensive, factual-based ratings, individual investors have to want to find the information they provide. We need mechanisms to drive demand by investors and consumers such that these sorts of ratings are a regular part of all informed decision-making. Most importantly we need to develop methods that ensure every type of investor has access to such information, which suggests that ESG considerations should become a regular part of all investment consultations between money managers and their clients. Money managers already move most clients toward long-term investment strategies, and in a manner of speaking, ESG principles are truly about the long-term impact of investment decisions. Investors, whether they are large entities with sizable equity involvement, employees participating in retirement savings funds, or individuals placing money in mutual funds, deserve to make investment decisions in a fully informed manner.

With transparent and readily available access to ESG ratings, then the real free market can exert its strength. It is important to acknowledge that impact investing does not have to be an all-or-nothing affair for investors. While obviously we want to see ESG investing–based decisions grow in popularity so that we can do greater good for more people, a starting point is to provide investors the full-market analysis that supports their making blended investment approaches divided among those that maximize their profit and those that accomplish mission-driven objectives. Much of the time, what a fully informed approach to investing will reveal is that the outcomes are not mutually exclusive, for the history of CDFIs offers clear evidence that their low-risk principles can make for quality returns even during unpredictable economic periods. Jed Emerson, the author of *The Purpose of Capitalism* and other books, came up with the blended-value concept that suggests portfolios don't have to be filled entirely with profit-maximizing investments. Yet one roadblock to making blended-value investments is the current system for assessing the performance of money managers because currently they are measured by their return against any of several indexes. It is beyond time that they also be measured by an additional set of benchmarks including the sorts of data sets employed by MSCI. Most of MSCI's benchmarking is related to environment. The challenge in ESG is benchmarking social enterprise. Much more work is needed here so that investors can compare social impacts across investment options.

It is worth remembering that the advent of mutual funds that have given rise to additional vehicles like exchange-traded funds and index funds first came onto the American scene with any significance in the late 1920s and were largely created as mechanisms for people of low income and those with low liquidity to essentially pool their money as a means into capital markets. Regulations regarding them were a central part of the Securities Act of 1933, and the Securities and Exchange Act of 1934 was highly focused on protecting people from unscrupulous investors who might target the vulnerable or poorly educated. Participation in such investment structures was common enough among the not-so-well-to-do that the term "widow-and-orphan stock" emerged, referring to equity investments that paid a high dividend while being considered low risk. They continue to exist and tend to focus investment in large, mature, stalwart companies in noncyclical business sectors. Some would argue, however, that a lot of modern regulation has skewed the investment market to high-net-worth individuals. Particularly in a climate that has seen such a long period of low interest rates that move sophisticated investors out of bond funds and beyond traditional bank-housed savings accounts and into equities, we have essentially created a de facto investment culture that shuts its door on large segments of the population. Simultaneously, we have created a culture where people are more expectant of having access to services without a middleman and certainly without being dependent on "authority management," something that has driven the equalitarian culture initiated by tech companies and the demand for commission-free trading, among other trends. It is a prime market in which to expand access to participation in social enterprise funds and tax-credit programs.

Many of my suggestions may seem to go against convention. But as I have detailed, the desired outcomes driving many investors' decisions no longer fit what has long been convention. It's beyond time that we don't just encourage such disruptions to the status quo but that we build rules to support them. As I have argued, all of our financial markets are organized through informal and formal rules of conduct and bound by enforceable contracts; however, as I have also made clear, too often regulators have written the rules in such ways that whole groups are excluded from participating. That reality is abundantly clear for low-income populations and people of color, but on the investment side of the equation, one can argue that it has largely been true for a majority of investors as well. Yet despite rules like home mortgage disclosure laws that date back to the 1970s, transparency of actions by those in finance have not been sufficient to stop inequitable treatment. If we are to create true market disruptions that can provide better freedom of investment decision-making, we are going to need to rewrite many of the rules. Change must occur in each of the three sectors—public, private, and philanthropic—in order to scale the remedies to the size of the problem.

> **IF WE ARE TO CREATE TRUE MARKET DISRUPTIONS THAT CAN PROVIDE BETTER FREEDOM OF INVESTMENT DECISION-MAKING, WE ARE GOING TO NEED TO REWRITE MANY OF THE RULES.**

PUBLIC SUPPORT OF SOCIAL VENTURES AND THE NEED FOR GOVERNMENT

As I have made clear, government has an important role to play in the expansion of capital markets, and the agencies that represent the federal government have developed a framework that has given rise to CDFIs and reinforced their primary mission of serving low- and moderate-income people and places. This enforcement is principally carried out by the Treasury Department through the annual CDFI certification and recertification processes. In order to augment the importance that I have placed on investor access to ESG data, the kind of alteration to current regulation I would like to see includes mechanisms that could bring more opportunity to the average person to be part of the solution by investing in funds and securities that benefit the people that CDFIs are trying to serve. There needs to be some loosening of the regulations, particularly around public solicitation. I am an advocate for more democratization in the finance industry because even strong, de-risked programs like NMTC are not attractive to high-net-worth individuals because they find that the credit is devalued by having to pay the alternative minimum tax. We must get Congress to exempt investments in NMTC from that tax by changing the rules to make NMTC investments attractive to individual investors.

While there are rightful worries about the inefficiencies of government (or indeed of large bureaucracy of any kind), not only has history taught us about the need for regulated markets as I have shown, but we have also lived through recent severe disruptions that demonstrate how timely, aggressive government response can mitigate large-scale economic shocks. The COVID-19 pandemic offered clear evidence via the use of the PPP how impactful and successful government intervention in times of economic crisis can be. While certainly there were challenges for PPP loan providers and business owners alike, the program was tremendously successful and helped millions of small-business owners stay in business and prevented further panic at an already anxious time. According to SBA data, about 94 percent of PPP loans that were approved in 2020 had been forgiven by

December 2021.[86] While the PPP was a very specific program meant for very specific conditions, the larger, long-term success of SBA loan programs demonstrates the role government can have when working alongside private entities and philanthropic organizations, most especially as a guarantor. We have also plenty of evidence that federal and state tax credits, like the NMTC or the low-income housing tax credit (LIHTC), can create market-driven incentives for scaled investment that can prove valuable to investors and borrowers alike.

Specific to NMTC, there are commonsense measures that can be taken to improve it and other capital market opportunities for social ventures, starting with the aforementioned elimination of the alternative minimum tax. Secondly, there is an urgency to make NMTC permanent rather than the current need to reauthorize the program every year. And thirdly, we need to increase the annual amount available for allocation to $5 billion, and then index that to inflation. The credit enjoys strong bipartisan support, which is unique in this time of divided government.

Since NMTC was originally tied to an omnibus spending bill, perhaps that accounts for the origins of why it must be renewed each year. Programs like these should be formed through focused legislation and be made part of the tax code, not added as amendments or placed in the microprint of budget bills. This could help to avoid corrosive application of good ideas.

There are also key changes that could be made to one other market tool I have not discussed elsewhere. Federally guaranteed CDFI bonds emerged from federal legislation after the Great Recession. While CRF has been able to issue $1 billion in bonds, CDFI bonds have

---

86   Kiah Treece and Jordan Tarver, "Two Years Later, Was the PPP Worth It?" Forbes
      Advisor, April 24, 2022, https://www.forbes.com/advisor/business-loans/ppp-two-year-
      anniversary/#:~:text=According%20to%20U.S%20Small%20Business,a%20Bloomberg%20
      News%20analysis%20suggests.

the capacity to have far more significance than currently is the case, and I would like to see these bonds become more readily available to far more midsized and small CDFI borrowers. The program provides fixed-interest, long-term loans to CDFIs at the federal borrowing rate plus a small interest markup. This capital is critical to CDFIs that make long-term mortgages. It enables them to match their liabilities and assets. Since its inception the program has issued more than $2 billion in bond loans to twenty-five CDFIs. It is a no-cost program to the taxpayer and has experienced no defaults. However, the public is prohibited by current law from purchasing these safe and impactful bonds, since the only entity allowed to purchase them is the Federal Financing Bank.

My belief is that the bond guarantee program could be very useful but requires revision in order to modernize the program and to reach its full potential. Rather than get into a great deal of policy analysis here, I invite you to visit my website, where I offer a fuller explanation of the program and what I playfully refer to as Bond Guarantee 2.0 that captures my suggestions for reforms. You will find a QR code at the back of the book that will transport you to my website.

As with the CDFI bond guarantee program, we need to make commonsense adjustments to other investment tools that already work. For example, in late 2021 the Consumer Financial Protection Bureau announced rule-making efforts to make modifications to the 1071 section of the Dodd-Frank act to require more reporting on application data for commercial loans across a broad spectrum of lenders. For the first time, lenders will be required to collect and report on the racial and ethnic characteristics of borrowers in ways like the aforementioned Home Mortgage Disclosure Act. Defining racial or other characteristics of business ownership is tricky, however. The larger the business, the more difficult it is to untangle who precisely is a business owner, for even smaller businesses can have complex suben-tities. Sometimes we fall into the "Don't let the perfect be the enemy of the good" mindsets. Making loan decisions based on whether a business is 51 percent or 49 percent minority owned, for example, reduces the role its minority owners—no matter their ownership per-centage—can have on its mission.

In the realm of overdue commonsense, throughout finance we need to create the means for more people to have greater freedom of choice for investment. A rich opportunity for increasing intergenerational wealth in minority communities is through employee stock ownership programs (ESOPs) or worker cooperatives. Currently, the SBA requires personal guarantees from all individuals who own 20 percent or more of a business enterprise. Because few ESOPs and worker co-ops have any individuals who have a 20 percent or greater ownership interest in an enterprise, they don't qualify for SBA loan guarantees. Congress has asked the SBA to address this issue, and in the interim the SBA has agreed to create an interim remedy by allowing third parties to provide guarantees for loans to ESOPs and cooperatives. This may be a role that philanthropies could play, as foundations are increasingly using their unleveraged balance sheets to guarantee impactful loans and invest-ments. To reach the scale needed to advance ownership by workers and employees, the SBA should reexamine its policies regarding ESOPs and cooperatively owned ventures.

There are additional commonsense improvements required across the spectrum of CDFI products and services, including important revision that could make another SBA program better, in this case a pilot program called Community Advantage that allows CDFIs to make SBA-guaranteed business loans. As with the revisions I have suggested for the bond guarantee program, to best dig into the policy changes I propose for Community Advantage, I have placed a discussion on my website. There you will also find additional discussion of what I believe must be the focus of any transformation of the SBA: closing wealth gaps.

Similarly, creating tax incentives that pump more money into targeted markets, or developing attractive equity-based investments, the public sector has two critical potent assets that go far beyond any roles it plays through regulatory and rule-making actions: becoming the agent that can weld the private and philanthropic sectors together in vital partnerships and de-risking capital programs that can attract investment and thereby get money into larger-scale social enterprises.

NURTURING THE GROWING INTEREST IN SOCIAL ENTERPRISES WITH THE PRIVATE SECTOR

Joining with public entities, no scaled response to the capital needs of low-income and diverse communities is possible without significant participation from the private sector. Such participation can come in two primary forms: first by creating enticing de-risked investment opportunities and second by direct participation in marketplaces by corporations and other businesses that respond to the needs of underserved communities and that sponsor programs that educate and elevate employees from those origins. Acting on the second of these endeavors can take many forms, including ensuring that corporate boards and leadership teams reflect the demographics of the places and people they serve (reflecting elements of the "G" of ESG); doing business with partners, vendors, and customers from underserved communities; supporting organizations that represent the interests of such communities; and developing retail and other facilities that cater to the specific local demographics and that demonstrate cultural sensitivity.

In many sectors there has been significant movement on the "G" section of ESG, particularly through expanding diversity on corporate boards. This is a critical need. But it cannot stop with boards and must extend into senior management (and indeed throughout management structures). CDFIs are already far ahead of the curve on both counts, a reality that needs to be replicated at other financial institutions. Developing greater inclusiveness in corporate leadership must go hand in hand with the development of social enterprise within an organization, particularly in rooting out institutional policies and structures that result in bias or other negative consequences. One response to George Floyd's murder that we made at CRF was to create mechanisms for interrogating all our policies, practices, and processes to ensure that we were not unintentionally building hidden bias into our own products and credit procedures. While this is an ongoing process at CRF, I'd encourage every enterprise to do the same and develop comprehensive internal audits to identify and root out unintentional bias in its credit practices.

In the spirit of capitalism, private enterprise must also simply acknowledge that there is financial gain to be realized by better meeting the needs of *all* communities. In short, while I do wish to encourage corporate social responsibility and believe that such a humanistic vision of business conduct is galvanized through genuine respect for others, it is in the interests of private enterprise to help shrink the wealth gap and benefit from the business opportunities that will result.

The disruptions that occurred because of COVID-19 are instructive, including the realization that the future is likely to result in more onshore investment in strategic industries like chip making and electronic battery manufacturing, among others, and with investment in worker education and reeducation, we are likely to see new workforce opportunities that, if centered in communities suffering from under-employment and stagnant advancement opportunities, could benefit workers and private enterprise alike. Onshore investment opportunities will arrive within an ecosystem that includes revision to the Community Reinvestment Act, which will feature increased emphasis on racial diversification in business lending supported by greater data collection on the racial characteristics of business borrowers. Many of those in private enterprise are already ahead of this curve and recognize that if they do not collect data, they cannot measure transformations that are occurring in their marketplaces. Others are wise to get on board quickly. It's certain that enlightened potential investors will already be savvy about expanding opportunities as more people are brought into financial markets.

One of the critical needs is to link private enterprise and private investors to CDFIs. There is a growing number of high-net-worth families and individuals that are handing over the management of family assets to millennial members for whom socially responsible investment is a priority. For example, at CRF we have been working with one group that has about six thousand global accredited investors representing $750 billion in assets. We need to make certain that such investors understand that CDFIs have developed the infrastructure to represent their interests in an ideal manner.

CDFIs are also uniquely positioned to assist large corporations in fulfilling the commitments so many made in the wake of George Floyd's murder. With over $50 billion in corporate commitments sparked by alignment with the interests of Black Lives Matter and other organizations, yet with only about 1 percent of those commitments deployed, we need these companies to better employ the expertise of CDFIs in getting capital onto the street. The risk is that, while genuine, such commitments reveal aspirations of corporate leaders, but the reality is that acting on those commitments is not their day job. If a C-suite executive is not continually pushing for fulfillment of the company's social justice initiatives, as always in business, other things and other moments of crisis arise, as we've seen in the economic woes throughout the pandemic. Partnerships with CDFIs can not only tap our expertise; they can also sustain momentum. CDFIs have the experience integral to qualifying such vendors and are adept at creating mechanisms to get them working capital so that they can reach the scale required. Corporations are increasingly showing the will to alter their own behaviors and act on ESG principles, but they have little expertise in doing so, particularly when it comes to helping lift up communities where access to capital has been historically unavailable. If they place their considerable influence—and their investment capital—into relational partnerships with CDFI and community development corporations, they can maximize their impact. But they need places to invest, particularly through their foundation arms.

Another opportunity to expand private enterprise involvement in underserved communities is through franchise ownership. There is very little risk in well-vetted franchises, so it is important that franchise parent companies look to expand diversity of ownership and locations of their franchises. It is important to note that not all franchises fall into the accusations sometimes leveled at them that they are extractive of low-income communities, particularly among fast-food enterprises. In actuality there are any number of franchise models that do not fit such controversial profiles, from window-washing companies to carpet-cleaning franchises to wellness facilities, among many others, that can create lucrative businesses where many of the costs associated with branding, marketing, and operations are carried by the parent company.

These are just a few of the areas in private enterprise that can be expanded upon in order to make scaled change happen. And it may well prove that private enterprise must lead the charge, for there is increasing evidence that more corporations are assembling governing structures and mandating policies that can benefit previously underserved communities. The simple reality is that as more large corporations take significant, sustained, genuine socially responsible action and invest both directly in underserved communities and through partnerships with entities like CDFIs, their size and influence serve as a potent impetus for others to follow suit. Moreover, they have the ability to take action quickly without descending into the political quagmires of inaction so common in the public sector.

MAXIMIZING THE LEVERAGE OF MISSION-DRIVEN PHILANTHROPY

Of course, the reduction of financial risk cannot occur without partnership with the philanthropic sector. Virtually none of the important work we have accomplished at CRF, like other CDFIs, would have been possible without the generous involvement of philanthropic entities. Beginning with the founding of CRF, partnership with foundations and charitable organizations has been critical for de-risking investments. Together, we have accomplished a great deal, yet we have not approached the scale that is required. What is still needed, and what is slowly beginning to take hold, is mission-driven investing models in the philanthropic world, which includes commitments by several leading foundations to leverage the abundant capital of their balance sheets. The vision they have shown essentially takes the model that we have successfully developed over the past thirty years and places it on steroids. A key element in scaling mission-driven investment is for foundations to move beyond investment of their endowments in traditional conservative investment portfolios to allow them to give away at least 5 percent of their endowments annually. Many foundations are finding ways to greatly expand their impacts by making program-related investments (PRIs). These PRIs help the full impact of their capital be realized by investing not just money earmarked for grants, but money from their evergreen endowments. CDFIs have a responsibility to educate foundation and charitable organizational boards and executives to demonstrate the sustainable success they can realize through PRIs and the "recycling" effect their giving can have. Such approaches can allow foundations and charities to do more for the core populations and causes that heralded their origins. Mission-related investments are those where the objective is essentially to achieve both financial and nonfinancial returns simultaneously. The nonfinancial returns can be in the form of social or environmental impact that directly aligns with the mission or the social beliefs of the organization.

In order to commit to leveraging their balance sheets, discussions are required among foundation boards addressing an expanded definition of their "prudent" fiduciary responsibilities, for in addition to assuming legal responsibility for the money foundations manage, their core purpose is to achieve specific philanthropic goals. Therefore, it is perfectly in keeping with the concept of fiduciary prudence—discharging duties solely in the interest of the participants and beneficiaries with the care, skill, prudence, and diligence under the circumstances then prevailing that a prudent person acting in a like capacity and familiar with such matters would use in the conduct of an enterprise of a like character and with like aims[87]—to include "prudent"

---

87 Cornell Law School, "29 U.S. Code § 1104. Fiduciary Duties," https://www.law.cornell.edu/uscode/text/29/1104.

care in the context of climate change and closing the racial wealth gap. Once we admit the role of human responsibility for climate change and the ethical responsibility to create equal opportunities for all humans to pursue life, liberty, and happiness, is it not prudent for those in fiduciary roles to take financial actions on the behalf of those whose lives will benefit from those actions?

I also think we need to clarify and expand such definition of fiduciary responsibilities as it applies to the prudent experts who manage retirement funds. For most in the middle class, their primary if not their only avenue for investing in capital markets is their 401k. Shouldn't all have the right to select funds and investment strategies that reflect their personal values? Is it "prudent" for fund managers to invest in industries that put human lives at risk or that are dependent on workers paid wages that keep them below the poverty level? There are trillions of dollars in retirement funds that could

THE KEY TO EXPANDING THE IMPACT OF INVESTMENT IS CREATING GREATER VELOCITY IN MOVING CAPITAL INTO THE HANDS OF THOSE ENTREPRENEURS AND COMMUNITY LEADERS WHOSE GOOD IDEAS HAVE BEEN DISMISSED BECAUSE THEY HAVE BEEN KEPT OUTSIDE TRADITIONAL MARKET STRUCTURES FOR TOO LONG.

be put to work for solving problems. Having proven that there are mechanisms by which we can de-risk social investments in a manner that maintains traditional fiduciary responsibility, do we not live in an age where we are capable of recognizing that we all share in social and environmental responsibilities as well? Most certainly those pensioners for whom managers are fiduciarily responsible should be able to readily access informed information about the full spectrum of investment options and be able to guide their managers into socially responsible investments if so inclined.

Those in philanthropic enterprises increasingly see new means to increase their impact and support the good work that is at the root of their purpose. The larger financial investment sector can learn from their successes and follow their lead. The key to expanding the impact of investment is creating greater velocity in moving capital into the hands of those entrepreneurs and community leaders whose good ideas have been dismissed because they have been kept outside traditional market structures for too long. Partnering with public and private entities alongside the CDFIs that can help them achieve such velocity, philanthropies form the bedrock on which we can build a larger, more just economy.

THE ROLE OF EDUCATION ABOUT SOCIAL ENTERPRISES

Every entity, large and small, public, private, and philanthropic, working in collaboration with others who share its mission, has a role in advocacy and guiding public policy. There is strength in numbers, and the very kinds of collaboratives and cooperatives that form community and that can link diverse approaches to positive change need to participate in the forums that represent their interests at all levels of public discussion and within government.

To accomplish such aims, for starters CDFIs must do a better job of heralding their good work. In a climate where more people are aligned with the missions of CDFIs, they need to be made more aware of their existence and know how they can participate not just as investors but as consumers who support the businesses and the communities they fund. Perceptions about social ventures are rapidly changing for the better, and CDFIs need to make a concerted effort to educate others in the financial industry. This must be paralleled with efforts to educate individuals who can benefit from the loans provided by investment instruments to know more about what is available to them to fund their enterprises.

Any attempt to educate money managers will be fruitless unless they and others in turn try to educate investors, whether those are individuals wishing greater control of their retirement accounts or corporate-scale investors. People's relationship to money is formed by how they were raised and how they were educated. We don't have a public education system that really educates people on money management. We need a concerted effort in public education to make financial literacy part of the curriculum. This must include understanding the time value of money and learning about the kinds of tools that can be employed to generate wealth over the course of a lifetime. We need parallel education for adults. CRF spends a great deal of effort sharing best practices and options for its borrowers, who are often new to the business lending world. Trusted guidance needs to be an expansive part of what all financial institutions do as well, and such programs can no longer only focus on those few individuals who already have an excess of wealth to invest.

Of course, those passing laws and those making or enforcing the rules need education as well, and an ongoing part of CDFI advocacy efforts must look ahead to new applications of existing products and services and to new, innovative mechanisms for creating velocity in credit markets. It is human nature to look backward to the last scandal or the most recent economic collapse and focus all attention on repairing the damage and making sure it is not repeated. Governments are no different in this way. Yet what is needed is far greater time invested in planning for future financial tools and anticipating shifting market conditions. We must address the myopic thinking I discussed at the outset of the chapter. No one can be a perfect prognosticator, but we must be better at focusing on innovation, bringing CDFIs and their borrowers into the digital economy, and conducting purposeful disruptions. In this regard trying to develop successful financial tools for the social enterprises of the near future is rather like planning for the next potential pandemic. Of course, we must respond to the crisis of the moment, but we must do so in a way that applies the lessons of the past and recognizes that new crises will arise. That understanding is not lost on people with fewer resources, for whom life can often seem a continuous series of unexpected events that create what seems an elongated downward spiral.

And yet, having reached this point of this book, I hope you also see that downward spirals are not inevitable, that proper intervention can create real opportunities for individuals—even whole communities—to change course. What we do know for certain is that when we do not invest in communities, we ensure their outcomes.

What if instead we all participated in ensuring entirely different outcomes? Everything we have accomplished at CRF has started with carefully cultivated relationships and the formation of partnerships. Our nexus approach of linking philanthropic organizations, private investors, and government-sponsored programs remains the force that creates entropy for our work. As we have succeeded in adapting to market needs over the course of our history and have earned approval by regulators and ratings agencies, we have been able to attract larger and more diverse partners. Our mindset must change. CDFIs have long had limited access to capital. We have thought in millions of dollars. True change will come only when low-income communities have access to billions, even trillions, of dollars. For CDFIs to operate at such a scale helping to develop commerce, fund educational and health facilities, and accelerate the wealth generation through business, homeownership, and ownership of other financial assets, we must form new partnerships and expand existing ones.

Bringing more people into capital markets as investors and as borrowers is more important than ever. Over the last fifty years, we have created a more stratified economic structure than ever, with fewer people controlling the vast majority of wealth and a seemingly intractable financial underclass that has been locked out of full participation in the economy. This reality parallels a larger dichotomous world culture where divisions are stark. Yet it is also an age in which more and more investors, particularly among the generation now entering the workforce, want control and influence over how their money is invested, largely in part because they see direct connections to the impact of their actions on the global environment and on the lives of those of lesser means. Their ethical desire for justice can generate the momentum we need to dismantle systemic roadblocks and presents a unique moment of opportunity. We dare not waste it. Those who can benefit from an expanded vision of capitalism are, after all, our neighbors, and it is only in working together that we can realize the kind of vibrant, healthy, sustainable communities that have always been the promise of American capitalism.

OUT OF MANY WE ARE ONE

I have shared before that one of the responses at CRF to the murder of George Floyd in our home city of Minneapolis was to interrogate our processes and policies to make certain we were not unintentionally creating any unjust or inequitable outcomes. To further that interrogation, we conducted implicit bias and racial equity workshops with our staff, which is an important starting ground for any organization. Of course, the systemic problems we face if we are to improve the outlook for those long excluded from access to capital require innovative, comprehensive solutions. I believe that an excellent framework for thinking about how best to envision the landscape of such solutions is found in a powerful metaphor found on the website for the Racial Equity Institute.[88] I cannot capture the full complexity or nuance of their metaphor, but here is its essence: Imagine that you are trying to rehabilitate a lake in which all the fish are dying. Now, you could, one by one, spend a lifetime trying to treat the fish, and perhaps you would save a few, but the conditions killing them won't be changed, and fish

---

88   Deena Hayes-Greene and Bayard P. Love, *The Groundwater Approach: Building a Practical Understanding of Structural Racism* (Greensboro, NC: The Racial Equity Institute, 2018).

will continue to die. You could focus on treating the water, cleaning it of whatever agent is killing the fish, and you may expand your success yet feel disappointment that the measures you are taking must be continuously repeated, and the results are inconsistent. Or you could recognize that a lake is not a static environment and choose instead to concentrate your efforts on treating the groundwater that feeds it. Only then can you impact the entire larger ecosystem in such a way that fish (and all other aquatic life and other species dependent upon the water as a resource) thrive. If we fail to "treat" the underlying, systemic conditions that maintain inequity, we can never solve the problems to which they give rise. The proper distribution of capital into the hands of smart, hard-working, entrepreneurial-minded people begins to "treat the groundwater," as it were, making inroads on systemic problems that have been present across multiple generations and creating change that will impact generations to come.

> IF WE FAIL TO "TREAT" THE UNDERLYING, SYSTEMIC CONDITIONS THAT MAINTAIN INEQUITY, WE CAN NEVER SOLVE THE PROBLEMS TO WHICH THEY GIVE RISE.

As we plan for the future, we must also look to the past. Virtually every financial tool that CRF has used in its history had either never been used before or never been utilized in quite the way we employed it. There will be new inventions. And there will be reinvention. But there are lessons in the past as well. At the intersection of Thirty-Eighth Street East and Chicago Avenue South in Minneapolis, near where George Floyd was murdered, there is a living memorial that includes a large metal sculpture of a raised fist in the middle of the intersection. Its location places it among murals, crosses, and other tributes and remembrances, and the intersection continues to spark spontaneous gatherings and has become an ongoing repository of flowers and other offerings. People come from all over the world to stand in solidarity for racial justice, express their pain and hope, and pay respect to the names of those who died unjustly. These offerings continue to be received and tended to by local community members.

The living memorial is a reminder to me as well, at multiple levels. As I have shared, this site of George Floyd's death is in an area where CRF was leading a lot of business development along Lake Street and Franklin Avenue in the first years of our existence. That work greatly benefited the community and was an important showcase of our mission and our methodology. The redevelopment of the neighborhood involved far more than the Midtown Global Market, far more than the redevelopment of the Sears building as a whole, and far more than the redevelopment of the Honeywell headquarters building. One reminder that is triggered in me when I see the memorial is that no matter the success of these projects and the meaningful transformation they brought to the community, it is change that remains fragile. Not only were many of those businesses we funded along Lake Street and Franklin Avenue damaged or destroyed in the violent wake of George Floyd's murder and others succumbed to COVID-19 closures and disruptions, but his murder itself at the hands of police is the true reminder of how much work remains. There is one additional reminder: the hundreds of loans we originated, the flow of capital that we opened, succeeded in, if you will, cleaning the lake, but we failed to clean the groundwater.

"Cleaning the groundwater," rooting out the systemic presence of racial inequity, will require all of us. Rich and poor, Black and Brown and Asian and Native American and White, progressive and conservative ... it will take all of us working together to create a new, just version of capitalism that works for all.

ABOUT THE AUTHOR

Frank Altman is the founder of Community Reinvestment Fund, USA (CRF), an innovative national CDFI that is committed to collaborating with others to fill gaps in access to capital and grow the capacity and capability of the industry. Altman pioneered the development of a secondary market for community and economic development loans when he established the organization.

Since 1988 CRF has grown from a small Minneapolis firm to a national organization serving community-based lenders across the country. In partnership with a network of local community partners, CRF has funded $3.6 billion in loans to job-creating small businesses, community facilities, charter schools, and affordable housing projects in forty-nine states plus Washington, DC, and in nearly one thousand communities.

Altman is a founding member and first president of the board of directors of the New Markets Tax Credit Coalition and helped spearhead the creation of a federal tax credit to encourage private investment in low-income communities. He is also a member of the Center for Community Development Investors at the Federal Reserve Bank of San Francisco and an advisor to the Social Innovation Initiative at Brown University. Altman was also instrumental in helping create the Detroit Home Mortgage program, which helps qualified home buyers obtain or refinance a mortgage. His work has been featured in *Inc.* magazine, where he was named one of its Entrepreneurs of the Year, and he received Fast Company's Social Capitalist award. He has been named an Aspen Institute Fellow at the Aspen Ideas Festival. The Small Business Administration has also named him Financial Services Advocate of the Year.

Altman frequently shares his expertise with numerous social and financial organizations across the country, including Center for Community Development Securities of the Federal Reserve Bank of San Francisco, the Financial Innovations Roundtable, Wall Street Without Walls, and US SIF—the Forum for Sustainable and Responsible Investment, and the US SIF Foundation.

Prior to founding CRF, Altman served as assistant commissioner for financial management at the Minnesota Department of Energy and Economic Development, where he administered several loan programs designed to create jobs in energy-related industries, promote energy conservation in public and private buildings, and finance manufacturing facilities in small communities. He earned his bachelor of arts degree from Brown University and his master of arts degree from the University of Minnesota.

GET IN TOUCH

For more information about Frank Altman
and *A New Capitalism*, visit www.FrankAltman.com.